WHAT IS THE BOOK OF EZEKIEL?

Kids' Guides to God's Word Series

What Is the Book of Genesis?
What Is the Book of Exodus?
What Is the Book of Leviticus?
What Is the Book of Numbers?
What Is the Book of Deuteronomy?
What Is the Book of Joshua?
What Is the Book of Judges?
What Is the Book of Ruth?
What Is the Book of 1 Samuel?
What Is the Book of 2 Samuel?
What Is the Book of 1 Kings?
What Is the Book of 2 Kings?
What Are the Books of 1–2 Chronicles?
What Are the Books of Ezra & Nehemiah?
What Is the Book of Esther?
What Is the Book of Job?
What Is the Book of Psalms?
What Is the Book of Proverbs?
What Is the Book of Ecclesiastes?
What Are the Books of Song of Songs & Lamentations?
What Is the Book of Isaiah?
What Is the Book of Jeremiah?
What Is the Book of Ezekiel?
What Is the Book of Daniel?
What Are the Books of Hosea–Micah?
What Are the Books of Nahum–Malachi?

What Is the Gospel of Matthew?
What Is the Gospel of Mark?
What Is the Gospel of Luke?
What Is the Gospel of John?
What Is the Book of Acts?
What Is the Book of Romans?
What Is the Book of 1 Corinthians?
What Is the Book of 2 Corinthians?
What Is the Book of Galatians?
What Is the Book of Ephesians?
What Is the Book of Philippians?
What Are the Books of Colossians & Philemon?
What Are the Books of 1–2 Thessalonians?
What Are the Books of 1–2 Timothy & Titus?
What Is the Book of Hebrews?
What Is the Book of James?
What Are the Books of 1–2 Peter & Jude?
What Are the Books of 1-3 John?
What Is the Book of Revelation?

What Is the Book of

EZEKIEL?

Michael Whitworth

ISBN 978-1-971767-26-0

Published by Start2Finish
Bend, Oregon 97702
start2finish.org

Printed in the United States of America
30 29 28 27 26   1 2 3 4 5

CONTENTS

INTRODUCTION

Have you ever watched someone lose everything?

Not in a movie where you know the hero will bounce back by the final scene. Real loss. The kind where a family moves out of the house they grew up in because they can't afford it anymore. The kind where someone you know gets a diagnosis that changes everything. The kind where you can see it in a person's eyes that the world they built their life around just collapsed, and they don't know what comes next.

Now imagine that happening to an entire nation. All at once. And imagine you're a young priest who was supposed to spend his life serving God in the most beautiful building on earth, and instead you're sitting in the dirt beside an irrigation ditch in Babylon, surrounded by people who look as lost as you feel, wondering if the God you devoted your life to even exists anymore.

That's where the book of Ezekiel begins. And what happens next is the wildest, strangest, most devastating, and ultimately most hopeful book in the Old Testament.

WHERE WE ARE IN THE STORY

To understand Ezekiel, you need to know what went wrong.

God had made a covenant with Israel at Mount Sinai. He would be their God. They would be his people. He gave them laws, a land, a temple, and his presence. For centuries, despite constant failures, God held the relationship together. He sent prophets. He sent warnings. He sent second chances.

Israel used up every one of them.

The northern kingdom fell to Assyria in 722 BC. The southern kingdom, Judah, limped along for another 136 years, but the verdict was already written. King after king led the people into idol worship. The temple that was supposed to house God's presence became a museum of pagan gods. The priests were corrupt. The prophets lied. The leaders exploited the poor. And God, who had endured centuries of betrayal with extraordinary patience, finally said: enough.

In 605 BC, Nebuchadnezzar of Babylon marched into the region. In 597, he besieged Jerusalem, stripped the temple of its treasures, and deported thousands of Judah's best and brightest to Babylon. Among those exiles was a thirty-year-old priest named Ezekiel.

Five years later, sitting by the Kebar canal in Mesopotamia, Ezekiel saw the sky tear open. And his life was never the same.

WHAT THIS BOOK IS ABOUT

Ezekiel is about the presence of God.

That might sound simple, but it drives everything in the book. In his opening vision, Ezekiel sees God's glory arriving in Babylon on a supernatural throne carried by living creatures, proving that God is not trapped in the Jerusalem temple. In the middle of the book, Ezekiel watches in horror as God's glory slowly, reluctantly departs from that same temple because the people have filled it with idols. And at the end, Ezekiel sees the glory return to a new temple, filling it forever, with a river of life flowing out from it to heal the world.

Glory arrives. Glory departs. Glory returns. That's the arc of the entire book, and it's really the arc of the entire Bible.

Along the way, Ezekiel does things no other prophet does. He lies on his side for over a year. He shaves his head and burns the hair. He builds a model city and besieges it with toy soldiers. He digs through walls, packs exile bags, and cooks bread over a fire fueled by dung. He is told his wife will die and that he cannot mourn. Every one of these bizarre actions is a sermon without words, a living demonstration of what God is about to do to Jerusalem.

Ezekiel also delivers some of the most creative and devastating speeches in Scripture. Allegories about unfaithful brides, useless vines, and two great eagles. A history of Israel told as three cycles of rebellion. Funeral songs for fallen kings and sunken ships. Oracles against nations from Ammon to Egypt. And then, when the judgment is finished and the city has fallen, some of the most beautiful promises in the Old Testament: a new heart, a new spirit, dry bones rising to life, a good shepherd searching for lost sheep, and a covenant of peace that will never end.

WHAT YOU'RE ABOUT TO READ

This book walks through Ezekiel in ten chapters, following the flow of the biblical text.

Chapters 1–3 cover Ezekiel's dramatic call and his overwhelming vision of God's throne.

Chapters 4–7 follow the prophet through a series of strange sign-acts that predicted the siege and destruction of Jerusalem.

Chapters 8–11 take Ezekiel on a visionary tour of the Jerusalem temple, where he discovers why God is about to leave.

Chapters 12–17 expose the lies of false prophets and tell three unforgettable allegories about Israel's guilt.

Chapters 18–20 tackle the question of individual responsibility and retrace the whole ugly history of Israel's rebellion.

Chapters 21–24 build to the worst day of Ezekiel's life: the beginning of the siege and the death of his wife.

Chapters 25–32 turn outward, announcing God's judgment on the nations that mocked Israel's fall.

Chapters 33–34 recommission Ezekiel as a watchman and condemn the selfish shepherds of Israel, with God promising to shepherd his people himself.

Chapters 35–37 contain the famous vision of the valley of dry bones and the promise of new hearts and God's Spirit.

And chapters 38–48 close the book with the defeat of a final enemy, a visionary temple, a river of life, and a city whose name says it all: "The Lord Is There."

WHY THIS MATTERS FOR YOU

You might be thinking: this sounds intense. And dark. And weird. Why should I read it?

Because Ezekiel answers questions you're already asking.

What do you do when life falls apart and God feels absent? Ezekiel was there. He sat in the dirt of exile and watched the sky open. God showed up where no one expected him.

How serious is sin, really? Ezekiel will show you. Not with abstract theology, but with burning hair and boiling pots and a glory cloud moving slowly toward the exit. Sin cost Israel everything. It cost Ezekiel his wife. It cost God his temple. Sin is not a small thing.

Does God actually care about me as an individual? Chapter 18 says yes. You are not trapped by your parents' failures. Your past does not define your future. God judges each person by the direction they're heading, and he takes no pleasure in the death of anyone. "Repent and live!" is his constant plea.

Can anything that's truly dead come back to life? Chapter 37 answers with a valley full of bones standing up and breathing. The God of Ezekiel specializes in the impossible. Dead nations. Dead hopes. Dead relationships. Dead faith. He breathes life into all of it.

And at the very end, what does God want? He wants to be with his people. The entire book builds toward a city named "The Lord Is There." Every judgment, every promise, every vision points to this one destination: God dwelling with us. Not distant. Not angry. Not absent. Present.

That's where the story of Ezekiel ends. And it's where the story of the Bible ends too. The last two chapters of Revelation describe a city with no temple, because God himself is the temple. A river of life flows from his throne. The leaves of the trees are for the healing of the nations. And God dwells with his people forever.

Ezekiel saw it first.

BEFORE YOU BEGIN

This book doesn't skip the hard parts. Ezekiel contains graphic language, intense imagery, and descriptions of judgment that can be unsettling. That's because God didn't skip the hard parts either. He told Ezekiel the truth about what was happening and why, even when the truth was painful. Every chapter in this book will explain what's going on and why it matters, not just for ancient Israel, but for you.

The God who speaks in Ezekiel is the same God who sent his Son. The glory that departed from the temple is the same glory that arrived in a manger. And the river that flows from God's throne in Ezekiel's final vision is the same river that flows through the last pages of Revelation.

So here we are, about to sit down beside a young priest at an irrigation canal in Babylon. He's lost his home, his career, and his future. He thinks the story is over.

He's about to find out it's just beginning.

Turn the page.

1

THE THRONE ABOVE THE STORM

Have you ever moved somewhere new and felt completely forgotten? Maybe your family relocated to a different state, and suddenly everything familiar was gone. Your old school, your friends, your bedroom, the route you used to walk without thinking. You're sitting in an unfamiliar house in an unfamiliar town, and for a moment you wonder if anyone back home even remembers you exist. You start to think that maybe all the things you were promised, all the plans you had for your life, died the day the moving truck pulled away.

Now imagine that feeling, but a thousand times worse. Imagine being ripped from your homeland by a foreign army, marched hundreds of miles across the desert, and dropped in a flat, muddy river plain in the middle of Babylon, the most powerful empire on earth. Imagine being a young priest who had trained your whole life to serve God in the Jerusalem temple, only to watch that dream evaporate when enemy soldiers put you in chains and dragged you away. Imagine sitting by a canal called the Kebar, surrounded by fellow exiles who all share the same hollow look in their eyes, wondering the same terrible question: *Has God forgotten us?*

That's where we find Ezekiel when this book begins. He's about thirty years old, which means something important. In Israel, thirty was the age when a priest officially began serving in the temple. This should have been the most important year of Ezekiel's professional life. Instead of stepping into the temple in Jerusalem, he's sitting in the dirt beside a Babylonian irrigation ditch, five years into exile, watching his calling disappear.

And then the sky splits open.

THE STORM AND THE THRONE

What Ezekiel sees next is the most overwhelming vision in the entire Old Testament. It is so intense, so far beyond anything he has words for, that his description stumbles and lurches as he tries to capture it. He piles up comparisons: "it looked like," "it appeared to be," "something resembling." He's not being vague on purpose. He's a man trying to describe the indescribable.

It started with a storm rolling in from the north. Not an ordinary storm. A massive cloud, churning with fire, flashing with lightning, surrounded by a brilliant glow. And from the heart of that fire came something that gleamed like molten metal in a furnace.

Out of the fire emerged four living creatures. They had a basic human shape, but everything else about them was strange and terrifying. Each one had four faces: a human face in front, a lion's face on the right, an ox's face on the left, and an eagle's face in the back. Each had four wings. Two wings stretched out to touch the wings of the creature beside it, forming a kind of living square. The other two wings covered their bodies. Their legs were straight, and their feet gleamed like polished bronze.

If you're having trouble picturing this, you're not alone. So was Ezekiel. But these creatures weren't random. They would have made more sense to someone living in the ancient world than they do to us. Massive sculptures of winged creatures with human faces guarded the entrances to Babylonian and Assyrian palaces. Ezekiel would have walked past figures like these, carved in stone, standing 10–16 feet tall at the gates of Babylon. The lion, the ox, the eagle, and the human were the most powerful and majestic beings in their respective realms. Together on one creature, they represented total, unlimited power.

And they were not the main attraction.

Beneath the creatures, Ezekiel noticed wheels. Not ordinary wheels. Each one appeared to be a wheel inside a wheel, able to move in any direction without turning. Their rims sparkled with what looked like jewels. And wherever the creatures moved, the wheels moved with them, perfectly synchronized, as if some invisible force was guiding them both.

Above the creatures was a platform that shimmered like crystal. And above the platform was a throne made of what appeared to be lapis lazuli, one of the most precious blue stones in the ancient world.

And on the throne sat a figure.

Ezekiel can barely bring himself to describe it. He says the figure looked like a human being, but everything about it radiated with impossible brilliance. From the waist up, it glowed like amber surrounded by fire. From the waist down, the same blazing light. The whole image was wrapped in a radiance that reminded Ezekiel of a rainbow.

And then he understood what he was seeing.

This was the glory of the Lord.

Ezekiel did the only thing a human being can do in a moment like that. He fell facedown on the ground.

GOD IN ENEMY TERRITORY

Think about what just happened. Ezekiel was sitting in Babylon, the territory of Marduk, the chief Babylonian god. In the ancient world, people believed that gods were tied to their land. If your nation was conquered, it meant your god had been defeated. The fact that Judah had fallen to Babylon seemed like proof to everyone, including many Israelites, that Marduk was stronger than the God of Israel.

But here was the God of Israel, arriving uninvited in the heart of Babylon on a throne carried by supernatural creatures, blazing with a glory that made the sun look dim. He hadn't been captured. He hadn't been defeated. He had come to Babylon on his own terms, moving freely in any direction he pleased, because no territory on earth is outside his reach. The wheels could go anywhere. The four faces looked in every direction. The whole vision was God's way of saying: *I am not limited to a building in Jerusalem. I go where I choose. And I have chosen to come here, to you, in this place where you think I've abandoned you.*

For a priest who thought his life was over, this was everything.

SENT TO A REBELLIOUS PEOPLE

But God didn't show up just to be seen. He showed up to speak. While Ezekiel was lying facedown, he heard a voice. "Son of man, stand up on your feet, and I will speak with you." That phrase, "son of man," simply means "human." God would use it to address Ezekiel over ninety times throughout the book. It was a constant reminder of the gap between them: you are mortal, and I am God. But it was also strangely tender. God was not speaking to a title or a rank. He was speaking to a person.

Ezekiel couldn't stand on his own. The vision had flattened him. But then the Spirit of God entered him and lifted him to his feet. This detail matters. Ezekiel didn't muster the courage to stand before God through sheer willpower. God gave him what he needed to stand. That's how it works throughout this book: God calls, and then God equips.

Once Ezekiel was standing, God gave him his assignment. And it was not a pleasant one. "I am sending you to the Israelites," God said, "to a rebellious nation that has rebelled against me. They and their ancestors have been in revolt against me to this very day. The people I am sending you to are stubborn and obstinate."

This was not a motivational speech. God didn't sugarcoat the mission. He described Israel as a "rebellious house" so many times in these opening chapters that it starts to sound like a title, as if God has renamed his people from "the house of Israel" to "the house of rebellion." And the message Ezekiel was supposed to deliver? Lament. Mourning. Woe. This wasn't a message of comfort. It was a message of coming disaster.

God also made something else clear: the people probably wouldn't listen. "Whether they listen or refuse to listen, they will know that a prophet has been among them." Ezekiel's job wasn't to be successful. It was to be faithful. He wasn't responsible for changing hearts. He was responsible for delivering the message.

But God didn't leave Ezekiel unprotected. He told Ezekiel not to be afraid of his audience, even though they would be like thorns and briars around him. Some have suggested that, in ancient Babylonian literature, being surrounded by thorns and scorpion plants was actually a picture of being untouchable, protected. God was building a wall around his prophet.

EAT THIS SCROLL

Then came the strangest part of the whole experience. Ezekiel saw a hand stretched out toward him, holding a scroll. The scroll was unrolled before his eyes, and he could see that it was covered in writing on both sides. The words were laments, mourning, and cries of grief. This was the content of Ezekiel's future ministry, summarized in three devastating words.

And then God told him to eat it. "Son of man, eat this scroll. Then go and speak to the house of Israel."

Ezekiel obeyed. He opened his mouth, and God fed him the scroll. He chewed it, swallowed it, let it fill his stomach. And when he did, something unexpected happened. It tasted sweet, like honey.

The sweetness didn't come from the content. The message on the scroll was nothing but sorrow. The sweetness came from the encounter itself, from the direct experience of receiving God's word. Even when God's message is painful, there is something deeply good about hearing from God at all. The scroll became part of Ezekiel. He didn't just carry the message. He *was* the message. From this point forward, when Ezekiel spoke, the words that came out would be the words God had placed inside him.

God then gave Ezekiel a second commissioning speech, reinforcing everything he had already said. He told Ezekiel that foreigners would have been easier to reach than his own people. Strangers who didn't even speak his language would have listened. But Israel, who knew the language of God's covenant, who had centuries of history with the Lord, would refuse. God promised to make Ezekiel's resolve as hard as the hardest stone, tougher than flint, so that the stubbornness of his audience would not crush him.

Then the Spirit lifted Ezekiel up. Behind him, he heard the thunderous sound of the living creatures' wings and the whirring of the wheels as the glory of the Lord rose from where it had been. The noise was like an earthquake. The vision was leaving. And Ezekiel was being carried back to his people.

SEVEN DAYS OF SILENCE

When he arrived at Tel Abib, the settlement where the Jewish exiles lived by the Kebar canal, Ezekiel sat down among them. And he didn't move for seven days.

The text says he sat there "overwhelmed." That word barely captures it. He was stunned, devastated, furious, grief-stricken. The scroll he had eaten was now doing its work inside him. He had swallowed a message of destruction for his own people, and it was tearing him apart. He was bitter. He was angry. He didn't want this job. The hand of the Lord was heavy on him, pressing him forward into a calling he would not have chosen.

Seven days of silence. Seven days of sitting among the people he had been sent to warn, unable or unwilling to speak. It was the posture of a mourner, the traditional period of grief in Israel. Ezekiel was mourning before the disaster had even happened, because he already knew what was coming.

After seven days, God spoke again. This time, he gave Ezekiel a title: watchman. In the ancient world, a watchman stood on the city wall and scanned the horizon for approaching enemies. When he spotted danger, he blew a trumpet to warn the people. If he sounded the alarm and they ignored it, their blood was on their own heads. But if he saw danger and stayed silent, God would hold him accountable for every life lost.

That was Ezekiel's role. Not a cheerleader. Not a motivational speaker. A watchman. His job was to see what God showed him and to say what God told him, whether anyone listened or not. The stakes were life and death, both for the people and for the prophet himself.

Then God imposed something remarkable. He told Ezekiel to go home and shut himself inside his house. He would be bound, and God would make his tongue stick to the roof of his mouth so that he could not speak freely. He would only open his mouth when God had a specific message to deliver. The rest of the time, silence.

This wasn't a punishment. It was part of the calling. Ezekiel was not a freelance preacher who could say whatever he wanted whenever he felt like it. He was God's instrument, and he would speak only God's words, on God's schedule. When God opened his mouth, he would say, "This is what the Sovereign Lord declares." When God was silent, Ezekiel would be silent too.

The prophet who had been called to speak would spend most of his time unable to.

WHAT THIS MEANS FOR US

First, God is not limited to the places where we expect to find him. Ezekiel was hundreds of miles from the temple, in a land considered unclean, surrounded by the worship of foreign gods. And God showed up in blazing glory. If you feel far from God right now, if your circumstances feel like exile, this vision says something important: God is not trapped in a building or a program or a comfortable season of your life. He goes where he wants, and he can reach you anywhere.

Second, God calls people who feel unqualified and unprepared. Ezekiel didn't volunteer for this. He didn't feel ready. He spent seven days sitting in silence because the weight of what God asked was too heavy to process. But God didn't wait for Ezekiel to feel confident. He gave him the Spirit, gave him the message, and gave him the strength to stand. If God is calling you to something that feels too big, that's normal. He doesn't call the equipped. He equips the called.

Third, faithfulness matters more than results. God told Ezekiel up front that his audience would not listen. That must have been discouraging. But God measured Ezekiel's success not by how many people responded but by whether he delivered the message. The same is true for you. You can't control how people respond to the truth. You can only control whether you speak it.

Fourth, God's word must be internalized before it can be shared. Ezekiel didn't just memorize a speech. He ate the scroll. The message became part of his body. Before you can offer anything meaningful to the people around you, God's truth has to get inside you. It has to shape how you think, how you feel, how you see the world. You can't give away what you don't have.

TALKING POINTS

1. **Ezekiel's vision of God came at the lowest point of his life, when he was in exile and had lost everything he'd planned for.** Why do you think God sometimes shows up most powerfully when life feels the worst? Have you ever experienced something good from God during a hard time?

2. **God told Ezekiel that his own people would be harder to reach than complete strangers.** Why do you think people who know the most about God are sometimes the most resistant to hearing from him?

3. **Ezekiel ate a scroll full of lament and mourning, and it tasted sweet.** What do you think this means? How can something painful also be good?

4. **God gave Ezekiel the title of "watchman" and told him he was responsible for delivering the warning, not for making people listen.** How does that change the way you think about sharing your faith or standing up for what's right? Does it take pressure off, or does it add a different kind of pressure?

5. **After his incredible vision, Ezekiel sat in silence for seven days, overwhelmed and bitter.** What does it tell you about God that he allowed Ezekiel to struggle with his calling instead of forcing him to immediately start preaching?

The vision faded. The thunder of the wings grew quiet. Ezekiel sat in the dust of Tel Abib with the taste of honey still on his tongue, the weight of God's hand still on his shoulders, and a message of destruction burning inside him.

He didn't want this job. But God hadn't asked for a volunteer. He had chosen a watchman. And the watchman had seen things that could not be unseen.

Now it was time to warn the city.

Turn the page.

2

A PROPHET WHO PREACHES WITHOUT WORDS

Walk into the British Museum in London, and you'll find a wall of stone panels taken from an ancient Assyrian palace. They're nearly three thousand years old, and they tell a story without a single word of text. Carved in stunning detail, panel after panel shows the Assyrian army besieging a city called Lachish, a fortress in the land of Judah. You can see soldiers pushing massive battering rams up earthen ramps toward the city walls. You can see archers raining arrows down from siege towers. You can see terrified families being marched out of the city gates as prisoners, carrying whatever they could grab. The carvings are so precise that archaeologists have traveled to the actual site of ancient Lachish and found the remains of that very ramp, still visible in the hillside after all these centuries.

King Sennacherib of Assyria was so proud of that conquest that he had the whole thing carved on the walls of his throne room. He didn't need to explain it. The images did all the talking.

Ezekiel was about to do something similar. God had called him to warn the Jewish exiles that Jerusalem was going to fall. But here was the problem: nobody wanted to hear it. The exiles in Babylon were clinging to hope that the city would survive, that the temple would stand, that they'd all be going home soon. Other prophets were telling them exactly what they wanted to hear. So God gave Ezekiel a different strategy. Instead of just speaking the warning, he would *act it out*. He would turn his own body, his diet, and his daily life into a living demonstration of what was about to happen to Jerusalem.

What follows in Ezekiel 4–7 is some of the strangest behavior recorded anywhere in the Bible. And every bit of it was deadly serious.

THE CITY ON A BRICK

God's first instruction was simple but attention-grabbing. "Take a clay brick and set it in front of you. Scratch a picture of Jerusalem on it."

Clay bricks were everywhere in Babylon. The whole city was built from them. And drawing maps on clay tablets was a common Babylonian practice. Archaeologists have found ancient city maps etched into clay, including one of the city of Nippur, the very region where the Jewish exiles were living. So when Ezekiel sat down in a public place and started scratching the outline of a city onto a brick, people would have gathered to watch. When they realized the city was Jerusalem, their hometown, they would have paid even closer attention.

Then Ezekiel did something that would have made their stomachs drop. He built a model siege around the brick. He piled up tiny mounds of dirt to represent siege walls. He constructed a miniature ramp, the kind attacking armies built to roll battering rams up to the city walls. He set up small camps around the model, representing enemy troops surrounding the city on all sides. And he positioned little battering rams aimed at the walls of his clay Jerusalem.

Anyone who had lived through a siege, or heard stories of one, would have recognized every detail. This was standard military strategy in the ancient world. Armies surrounded a city to cut off food and supplies, then built ramps and rolled up battering rams to break through the walls. The exiles had seen the Babylonian army do this to their own city just five years earlier.

But Ezekiel wasn't finished. He took an iron cooking griddle and placed it between himself and the brick city like a wall. Then he set his face against the model, glaring at it with hostility.

The message was devastating. The griddle represented an impenetrable barrier between God and Jerusalem. God wasn't just allowing the siege to happen. He was the one behind it. The iron wall meant that no prayer would get through. No cry for help would be heard. God himself had turned his face against his own city.

Then Ezekiel declared: "This is a sign for the house of Israel."

A sign. A living, visible warning of what was coming.

LYING DOWN FOR OVER A YEAR

The next act was even more extreme. God told Ezekiel to lie down on his left side and stay there for 390 days. Then he was to turn over and lie on his right side for 40 more days. Each day represented a year: 390 years of Israel's accumulated rebellion against God, and 40 years of punishment that would follow.

Think about that. Ezekiel lay on his side, day after day, for over a year. He probably wasn't lying down around the clock. He likely adopted this position during the busiest hours of the day, when the most people would see him, and then returned to his house in the evenings. But even so, the commitment was extraordinary. Day after day, week after week, month after month, the prophet lay on his side in front of his little model of besieged Jerusalem. His bare arm was stretched out toward the city in a gesture that looked like a warrior preparing for battle.

His neighbors would have walked past him every day. Some probably thought he was crazy. Others may have stopped and stared, trying to figure out what he was doing. But the message was clear to anyone willing to see it: the God of Israel had been patient for centuries, enduring generation after generation of rebellion. And that patience had finally run out. Judgment was no longer a possibility. It was a certainty. And it was going to last a long time.

STARVATION RATIONS

While Ezekiel lay on his side, God prescribed his diet. And it was miserable.

He was to take wheat, barley, beans, lentils, millet, and a coarse grain called emmer, mix them all together, and bake bread from the combination. This wasn't a recipe. It was scraping the bottom of every storage container you owned and combining whatever crumbs you could find. During a real siege, when food supplies ran out, people couldn't afford to be picky. You ground up whatever was left and made it into something barely edible.

His daily food allowance was about eight ounces, roughly the weight of a large apple. His daily water was about two-thirds of a quart. For comparison, a normal person needs about 64 ounces of water a day. Ezekiel was getting a fraction of that. This was a starvation diet, the kind of rationing that happens when a city has been under siege for months and the supplies are almost gone.

Then God told him how to cook the bread: over a fire fueled by human waste.

This is where Ezekiel, for the first and only time in the early chapters, pushed back. "No, Lord God!" he protested. "I have never defiled myself. From the time I was young until now, I have never eaten anything unclean. No contaminated food has ever entered my mouth." Ezekiel was a priest. His entire identity was built around ceremonial purity. Cooking food over human waste would violate everything he had been trained to protect.

God listened. And he made a concession. Ezekiel could use cow dung instead.

That might not sound like much of an improvement to us, but dried animal dung was actually a common fuel source in the ancient world, especially in places where wood was scarce. The point of the original command wasn't really about the fuel. It was about contamination. God was saying: this is what life will be like for my people when they are scattered among foreign nations. They will eat unclean food in unclean lands, cut off from the temple, cut off from proper worship, cut off from everything that made them who they were.

The exiles watching Ezekiel were already living this reality. They were already in a foreign land, already eating food prepared in ways that made a faithful Israelite uncomfortable. Ezekiel's diet was a mirror held up to their own situation, and a warning that things were about to get much worse for those still in Jerusalem.

THE SWORD AND THE HAIR

After the 430 days of lying on his side were complete, God gave Ezekiel one final dramatic instruction. He was to take a sharp blade and shave off all his hair, both his head and his beard. Then he was to divide the hair into three equal parts.

The first third, he was to burn in a fire right on top of his model of Jerusalem. The second third, he was to chop up with the blade all around the model city. The third portion, he was to scatter to the wind.

Each pile of hair represented a portion of Jerusalem's population. A third would die by fire and plague inside the city during the siege. A third would be cut down by the sword of the invading army around the city. A third would be scattered among the nations as refugees and exiles, and even there, some would be hunted down.

But before scattering that last portion, Ezekiel was to take a few strands and tuck them into the fold of his garment, close to his body. A tiny remnant, saved and carried close. Even in total destruction, God would preserve a handful. Not many. But enough.

For a priest, shaving your head was an act of mourning. It was also deeply humiliating. By the time Ezekiel stood before his neighbors, bald and beardless, surrounded by burned and scattered hair, with a miniature ruined city at his feet, the message could not have been more graphic. Jerusalem was going to be destroyed. Most of its people were going to die. And God was the one doing it.

WHY?

Chapters 5–7 provide the explanation. After all the sign-acts, God speaks directly, and his words are blistering. "This is Jerusalem, which I have set in the center of the nations." God had placed Jerusalem at the crossroads of the ancient world, at the meeting point of three continents, so that what he did there would be visible to everyone. Israel was supposed to be a showcase of what it looked like when a nation lived under God's blessing and followed his ways.

Instead, they had been worse than the surrounding nations. Worse than the people who had never known God at all. "She has rebelled against my laws and my decrees more than the nations and countries around her." The people who had received the most had done the least with it. The nation that was supposed to be a light to the world had become darker than the darkness around it.

So God declared the unthinkable: "I myself am against you." Not just disappointed. Not just withdrawing his protection. Actively hostile. The God who had rescued Israel from Egypt, who had parted the sea, who had fed them in the wilderness, who had given them the land, who had built his temple among them—that God was now their enemy.

The consequences described in chapters 5–7 are staggering in their severity. Famine so extreme that parents would eat their own children. The temple itself desecrated by invaders.

High places and altars where people had worshiped idols torn down and littered with the bones of the worshipers. The economy destroyed. The leadership stripped of power. Every source of guidance and protection removed. And over and over, the phrase that echoes like a drumbeat through these chapters: "Then you will know that I am the Lord."

That phrase appears dozens of times throughout the book of Ezekiel. It is the point of everything. Every act of judgment, every shattered idol, every broken wall was meant to accomplish one thing: to force a stubborn, blind, rebellious people to finally see who God really is. Not Marduk. Not Baal. Not the golden calves or the carved images or the sacred poles on the hilltops. The Lord. The only God. And a God who will not be ignored.

Chapter 7 closes the section with language that sounds almost like a funeral. "The end has come. The end has come upon the four corners of the land." It repeats the word "end" over and over, as if hammering a nail into a coffin. Money will be worthless. The temple will be violated. Prophets will have no visions. Priests will have no instruction. Elders will have no wisdom. Everything the people depended on will be stripped away until they have nothing left but God himself.

WHAT THIS MEANS FOR US

First, God will go to extraordinary lengths to get through to people who refuse to listen. Ezekiel didn't just preach sermons. He built models, starved himself, lay on his side for over a year, and shaved his head. God used every possible method to break through his people's stubbornness. If you feel like

God is being persistent with you about something, pay attention. He doesn't give up easily.

Second, privilege increases responsibility. Jerusalem's judgment was so severe precisely because Jerusalem had received so much. God had placed his name there. He had given them his law, his temple, his prophets. And they had squandered all of it. The same principle applies to anyone who has been given access to truth. Knowing what's right and choosing to ignore it isn't neutral. It's worse than never knowing at all.

Third, God's patience is real, but it has limits. The 390 years of accumulated sin that Ezekiel symbolized on his side represented centuries of God enduring rebellion, sending prophets, offering chances to repent. He is genuinely slow to anger. But "slow" is not the same as "never." There comes a point when the consequences of persistent rebellion can no longer be delayed.

Fourth, even in the worst judgment, God preserves a remnant. Those few strands of hair tucked into Ezekiel's garment represent God's refusal to let his people be completely destroyed. The remnant is tiny. The losses are catastrophic. But God always keeps a thread alive, because his promises depend not on human faithfulness but on his own.

TALKING POINTS

1. **Ezekiel used dramatic visual demonstrations instead of just words.** Why do you think actions can sometimes communicate more powerfully than speeches? Can you think of a time when someone's actions taught you something that words alone couldn't?

2. **God said Jerusalem had been "more unruly than the nations around her," meaning the people who knew God best had behaved worse than those who didn't know him at all.** Why do you think that happens? How can knowing the right thing actually make it harder to do the right thing?

3. **Ezekiel protested when God told him to cook over human waste, and God gave him an alternative.** What does this tell you about God's willingness to listen when we honestly struggle with what he asks? Is there a difference between protesting out of genuine conviction and simply refusing to obey?

4. **The phrase "then you will know that I am the Lord" runs through these chapters like a refrain.** What does it mean to truly "know" that God is the Lord? Is it possible to believe God exists without really knowing who he is?

5. **God preserved a tiny remnant, a few strands of hair tucked into Ezekiel's garment, even while destroying nearly everything else.** What does this teach you about how God balances justice and mercy? How does the idea of a remnant give you hope?

The demonstrations were over. The brick city lay in ruins. The hair was burned, scattered, and gone. The prophet stood bald and thin before his neighbors, a living portrait of what was coming.

But no one had seen anything yet. In his next vision, Ezekiel would be transported back to Jerusalem itself, and what he would see inside the temple walls would explain exactly why God's patience had reached its breaking point.

Turn the page.

3

GOD LEAVES THE BUILDING

One of the oldest and most famous stories in Western literature is the fall of Troy. For ten years the Greek army had camped outside the walls of the city, unable to break through. Troy's defenses were legendary. Its gates were massive. Its walls were thick. No amount of fighting could bring the city down from the outside.

So the Greeks tried something different. They built an enormous wooden horse, hid their best soldiers inside it, and left it at the gates as a supposed gift. Then they sailed away, pretending to give up. The Trojans celebrated. They dragged the horse inside the walls, threw a party, and went to sleep believing the war was over.

That night, the Greek soldiers crept out of the horse, opened the city gates, and let in the rest of the army. Troy burned. The city that no enemy could conquer from the outside was destroyed from within. The real danger had never been the army at the gates. It was the thing the people had willingly invited inside their walls.

Ezekiel 8–11 tells a similar story, except it isn't fiction, and the stakes are infinitely higher. In these chapters, God transports Ezekiel in a vision back to the Jerusalem temple, the holiest place on earth, the building where God's own presence dwelled. And what Ezekiel finds inside is so shocking, so revolting, that it explains everything that is about to happen to the city.

The enemy isn't outside the walls. The enemy is already in the sanctuary.

THE VISION BEGINS

About fourteen months after his first vision by the Kebar canal, Ezekiel was sitting in his house in Babylon. The elders of the exiled community had come to visit, probably hoping for a word from God about when they might go home. What they got instead was something none of them expected.

A figure appeared before Ezekiel, blazing with light, like fire from the waist down and glowing metal from the waist up. It was similar to the figure Ezekiel had seen on the throne in his first vision. Then the figure reached out something like a hand and grabbed Ezekiel by the hair. The Spirit lifted him up between earth and heaven and carried him, in the vision, all the way to Jerusalem.

Ezekiel's body stayed in Babylon. The elders were still sitting in front of him. But his spirit was standing at the north gate of the temple complex, about to see things that would haunt him for the rest of his life.

The first thing he noticed was a contrast that said everything. In one direction he could see the glory of the God of

Israel, the same blazing, radiant presence he had witnessed in Babylon. But right there, at the entrance to the temple, stood an idol. The text calls it "the idol that provokes to jealousy." We don't know exactly what this image was, though it may have been a statue of the Canaanite goddess Asherah. What we know is that it was sitting on God's property, right at the front door of his house, like a slap in the face.

And God said to Ezekiel: "Do you see what they are doing? Do you see the utterly detestable things the house of Israel is doing here, things that drive me far from my sanctuary? But you will see things that are even more detestable."

Even more detestable. That phrase will repeat like a warning siren through this entire vision. Every time Ezekiel thinks he's seen the worst of it, God says: keep looking.

FOUR ROOMS OF HORROR

What follows is a guided tour of the temple, and each stop is worse than the last. God leads Ezekiel through the complex like a prosecutor presenting evidence, building a case for judgment one exhibit at a time.

The secret room. God brought Ezekiel to a hole in the wall near the temple courtyard. "Dig through the wall," he said. Ezekiel dug and found a hidden doorway. When he went inside, he saw the walls covered with carvings of crawling creatures and detestable animals, images that may have reflected Egyptian religious practices. Standing before these images were seventy elders of Israel, each holding an incense burner, filling the room with fragrant smoke. These weren't nobodies. These were the leaders of the nation, the men responsible for guiding

God's people. And they were worshiping animal images in a secret room inside God's own temple.

One of them was Jaazaniah, the son of Shaphan. That name would have been a gut punch to anyone who knew Israel's recent history. Shaphan's family had been among the most faithful supporters of God's word during the reforms of King Josiah. His father had helped rediscover the Book of the Law in the temple. And now his son was leading secret idol worship in the same building.

The elders had convinced themselves that God couldn't see them. "The Lord does not see us," they whispered. "The Lord has forsaken the land." They believed that when Babylon conquered Judah, it meant God had been defeated or had simply left. So they turned to other gods, hedging their bets, covering their bases with the deities of the nations around them.

They were wrong about God leaving. He was right there, watching every move.

The women mourning Tammuz. God brought Ezekiel to the north gate of the temple, and there he saw women sitting and weeping for Tammuz. Tammuz was a Mesopotamian god, a figure from Babylonian religion whose followers believed he died each year when the summer heat scorched the land and rose again when the rains returned. His worshipers mourned his "death" with weeping and ritual laments, hoping to bring back fertility and rain.

This was Babylonian religion being practiced at the entrance to the Lord's temple. The women of Jerusalem had imported the worship of a foreign god and set it up right next to the place where the true God dwelled. They were crying over a dead idol while the living God stood ignored a few yards away.

The sun worshipers. God brought Ezekiel into the inner court of the temple, the area between the main entrance and the altar, a space normally reserved for priests. There he saw about twenty-five men with their backs to the temple, facing east, bowing down to the rising sun.

Think about the physical posture for a moment. The temple entrance faced east. To worship the sun as it rose, these men had to turn their backs on the temple, on the Holy Place, on the very room where God's presence dwelled. They were literally turning their backs on God in order to bow before a created object. The sun that God had made was being worshiped while the God who made it was being ignored. This was not just disobedience. It was a deliberate, public insult.

God's summary of the entire tour was devastating: "Is it a trivial matter for the house of Judah to do the detestable things they are doing here? They have filled the land with violence and have continually aroused my anger." And then: "Therefore I will deal with them in anger. I will not look on them with pity or spare them."

THE EXECUTIONERS

What happened next is one of the most terrifying scenes in the Bible. God called out with a loud voice, and six figures appeared, each carrying a weapon of destruction. With them was a seventh figure, dressed in linen and carrying a writing kit. This man in linen was the key to everything that followed.

God told the man in linen to go through the city of Jerusalem and put a mark on the foreheads of everyone who grieved over the sins being committed. Anyone who looked at what was happening in the temple and mourned, anyone whose heart was broken by the rebellion of their neighbors, that person would receive a mark of protection.

Then God gave the six executioners their orders: "Follow him through the city and kill. Show no mercy and no compassion. Slaughter the old, the young, women, and children. But do not touch anyone who has the mark. Begin at my sanctuary."

They began at the sanctuary. The very place that should have been safest became the starting point for judgment. The elders who had been worshiping images in the secret room were the first to fall.

Ezekiel watched in horror. He fell facedown and cried out: "Are you going to destroy the entire remnant of Israel in this outpouring of wrath on Jerusalem?" It was the cry of a mourner, the sound of a man who had swallowed a scroll of lament and was now living it. He pleaded for mercy.

God's answer was firm. "The sin of the house of Israel and Judah is exceedingly great. The land is full of bloodshed. The city is full of injustice. They say, 'The Lord has forsaken the land; the Lord does not see.' So I will not look on them with pity or spare them. I will bring down on their heads what they have done."

Then the man in linen returned and reported: "I have done as you commanded." The marking was finished. The few who grieved had been set apart. Everyone else was exposed.

THE GLORY DEPARTS

Now comes the moment the entire book has been building toward. It is the most devastating event in the Old Testament, and it happens in slow motion.

The glory of the Lord began to move.

Remember, God's glory had been dwelling in the temple since the days of Solomon. When Solomon finished building the temple nearly four hundred years earlier, the glory of the Lord had descended and filled the building so powerfully that the priests couldn't even stand to perform their duties. God had moved in. His presence was the whole point of the temple. Without it, the building was just stone and wood.

Now, for the first time, the glory began to leave.

It moved in stages, slowly, almost reluctantly, as if giving the people every possible moment to notice and repent. First the glory rose from above the cherubim on the ark of the covenant in the Most Holy Place and moved to the threshold of the temple. This was already catastrophic. God was stepping away from his throne on earth.

Then, as the cherubim from Ezekiel's first vision appeared again (the same living creatures, the same wheels, the same blazing light), the glory moved out of the temple entirely and took its place above the cherubim at the east gate of the temple complex. God was at the edge of his own property, pausing at the exit.

Before the glory departed completely, God delivered one more message. He condemned the leaders of Jerusalem who were telling people the city was safe, that Jerusalem was like a cooking pot that would protect the meat inside it. God corrected them: the "meat" in the pot wasn't the comfortable leaders. It was the innocent people those leaders had murdered. The leaders themselves would be dragged out of the city and judged at the borders of Israel. Their confidence in Jerusalem's invincibility was a lie.

Then, in a moment of stunning grace right in the middle of all this judgment, God turned his attention to the exiles. The people of Jerusalem had been mocking those in Babylon, saying, "They are far from the Lord. This land has been given to us." But God said the opposite was true. "Although I sent them far away among the nations, I have been a sanctuary for them in the countries where they have gone."

Did you catch that? God himself had become a sanctuary for the exiles. They didn't need a building. They had God. And God promised them something extraordinary: "I will give them an undivided heart and put a new spirit in them. I will remove from them their heart of stone and give them a heart of flesh." A spiritual heart transplant. New desires. New loyalty. A fresh start that no temple building could provide.

Then the glory of the Lord rose from the city and stopped on a mountain east of Jerusalem, the Mount of Olives. And there it paused, as if looking back one last time.

Then Ezekiel's vision ended. The Spirit carried him back to Babylon, and he told the exiles everything he had seen.

WHAT THIS MEANS FOR US

First, hidden sin is never actually hidden. The elders in the secret room thought God couldn't see them. They were wrong. God sees through walls and into hearts. You may be able to hide what you're doing from your parents, your friends, or your church. You cannot hide it from God. And the longer hidden sin goes unaddressed, the more damage it does.

Second, the worst threat to God's people has always been internal, not external. Babylon wasn't what destroyed

Jerusalem. Idolatry was. The people invited false gods into the one place that belonged exclusively to the Lord. The greatest dangers to your faith are rarely the obvious ones. They're the compromises you make quietly, the loyalties you divide, the things you let into spaces that belong to God.

Third, God's departure is the ultimate judgment. Worse than famine. Worse than war. Worse than exile. When God's presence leaves, everything else collapses. The temple without God's glory was just a building. The city without God's protection was just a target. The scariest thing that can happen to anyone isn't suffering. It's God stepping back and letting you have exactly what you chose instead of him.

Fourth, even in judgment, God protects those who grieve over sin. The man in linen marked everyone who mourned over what was happening. God noticed the people whose hearts were broken by the rebellion around them. He sees you when you care about the things he cares about, even when it feels like no one else does.

Fifth, God's presence is not tied to a building. "I have been a sanctuary for them," God said about the exiles. The people in Jerusalem thought they were safe because they had the temple. The exiles thought they were abandoned because they didn't. Both were wrong. God goes where he chooses, and he had chosen to be with the people in Babylon. His presence doesn't depend on an address. It depends on his love.

TALKING POINTS

1. **The elders in the secret room said, "The Lord does not see us; the Lord has forsaken the land."** Why do you think

people convince themselves that God can't see what they're doing? Have you ever been tempted to think that way?

2. **Each scene in Ezekiel's temple tour was worse than the one before: the idol at the gate, the secret room, the women mourning Tammuz, the men worshiping the sun.** Why do you think sin tends to escalate? How does one compromise lead to another?

3. **God told the man in linen to mark those who "grieve and lament" over the detestable things being done.** What does it look like to grieve over sin in your community without being judgmental or self-righteous?

4. **The glory of God left the temple slowly, in stages, almost as if giving the people time to notice.** What do you think this tells us about God's character? Is he eager to leave, or reluctant?

5. **God told the exiles, "I have been a sanctuary for them."** How does this promise change the way you think about God's presence? Can you experience God deeply even when you feel far from the places or circumstances where you'd expect to find him?

The glory hovered over the Mount of Olives, then it was gone. The temple stood empty. The building that had been the most sacred place on earth was now just stone, stripped of the presence that gave it meaning.

Centuries later, a man would stand on that same mountain, look out over that same city, and weep. "Jerusalem, Jerusalem," Jesus would say, "how often I have longed to gather your children together, as a hen gathers her chicks under her wings, and you were not willing." The glory that left in Ezekiel's day would one day return, not in a cloud, but in a person.

Turn the page.

4

LIES, VINES, AND EAGLES

Have you ever been told exactly what you wanted to hear, only to find out later it was a lie? Maybe a friend said your project looked great when it didn't, and you turned it in and got a bad grade. Maybe someone promised everything was going to be fine when it clearly wasn't, and you trusted them because the truth was too scary to face. Maybe you've been on the other side of it, telling someone what they wanted to hear because the truth felt too hard to say.

There's a strange comfort in a lie that tells you everything is okay. It lets you relax. It lets you stop worrying. It lets you pretend that the problem isn't real and that you don't need to do anything about it. The trouble is that the problem doesn't go away just because someone told you it wasn't there. The crack in the wall is still spreading. The storm is still coming. And when reality finally hits, the people who told you not to worry are nowhere to be found.

That's the situation in Israel during Ezekiel's time. The nation was dying, and almost everyone with a microphone was saying it wasn't. False prophets were telling the people that peace was coming, that Jerusalem would stand, that the exiles would be home soon. Meanwhile, Ezekiel was the one voice saying, "No. It's worse than you think. And you need to hear the truth before it's too late."

Ezekiel 12–17 is about what happens when a nation chooses comfortable lies over painful truth. It contains some of the most vivid, creative, and heartbreaking images in the entire book: a prophet digging through a wall in the dark, a crumbling structure covered in whitewash, a vine too useless even for a peg, a bride who becomes a prostitute, and two great eagles circling over a fragile vine. Behind all of it is one question: Will you listen to the truth, or will you keep believing the lie?

PACKED FOR EXILE

God told Ezekiel to perform another sign-act, this time aimed directly at the people's stubborn hope that the exiles would soon return to Jerusalem and everything would go back to normal.

During the day, in full view of his neighbors, Ezekiel packed a bag. Just the basics, the kind of bundle you'd grab if you were fleeing your home in the middle of the night. Then, after dark, he dug a hole through the wall of his house and crawled through it with his pack on his shoulder and his face covered so he couldn't see where he was going.

The next morning, when the curious exiles asked what he was doing, God gave the interpretation. This was a picture of King Zedekiah, the puppet ruler the Babylonians had installed in Jerusalem. When the city finally fell, Zedekiah would try to escape by night through a breach in the city wall. He would be caught. His sons would be killed in front of him. Then his eyes would be gouged out, and he would be taken blind to Babylon, where he would die.

That last detail is chilling when you read the prophecy carefully. God said Zedekiah would be brought to Babylon but would "not see it." At the time, that sounded like a contradiction. How could he go to Babylon and not see it? The answer came a few years later, when Nebuchadnezzar's soldiers put out Zedekiah's eyes before the march to Babylon. He arrived in the city but saw nothing. Ezekiel's prophecy was fulfilled down to the detail.

The exiles were watching Ezekiel crawl through a wall in the dark. What they were really watching was the future of their king.

THE WHITEWASHED WALL

After the sign-acts, God turned his attention to the people who were making Ezekiel's job nearly impossible: the false prophets.

These weren't worshipers of foreign gods. They claimed to speak for the Lord. They said, "Thus says the Lord," just like Ezekiel did. The difference was that God had never spoken to them. They were inventing their messages out of their own imaginations, telling people what they wanted to hear, and collecting payment for the service.

God's description of them was blistering. He compared them to jackals running through ruins, scavenging in the rubble of a collapsed building instead of doing anything to prevent the collapse. They hadn't "gone up to the breaches in the wall." In other words, they saw the cracks in the nation's spiritual defenses and did nothing. Worse than nothing. They covered the cracks with whitewash.

That image is the heart of the chapter. Picture a wall that's falling apart. The stones are loose, the mortar is crumbling, and the whole structure is leaning dangerously. A responsible builder would tear it down and rebuild it properly. But the false prophets just slapped on a coat of white plaster and said, "Looks fine! Nothing to worry about!"

God's response was vivid and furious. "I will send a violent wind. I will send torrential rain and hailstones. The wall will collapse, and you will be destroyed with it. Then people will ask, 'Where is the whitewash you covered it with?'" The cosmetic fix was worthless. When the storm hit, the wall would come down, and the people who had trusted it would be crushed underneath.

This wasn't just about ancient Israel. The principle is timeless. Whenever someone tells you that sin doesn't matter, that consequences aren't real, that God doesn't care how you live, they're whitewashing a crumbling wall. It might look nice for a while. But it won't stand.

God also condemned false prophetesses who practiced a kind of fortune-telling, using magic charms and veils to hunt down the souls of God's people like trappers catching prey. They told lies to the righteous and encouraged the wicked, and God promised to tear their snares apart and set the captives free.

IDOLS IN THE HEART

Then came a scene that revealed just how deep the problem ran. Some of the elders of the exiled community came and sat down in front of Ezekiel, presumably wanting a word from God. But God told Ezekiel something the elders didn't expect him to know: "These men have set up idols in their hearts."

They weren't carrying statues. They weren't bowing to carved images. The idolatry was internal. They had divided their loyalties between God and the gods of the nations around them. They were hedging their bets, trying to worship the Lord and hold onto pagan allegiances at the same time. And then they had the nerve to come ask God for guidance.

God's response was pointed: "Should I let them inquire of me at all?" His answer was a call to repentance. Turn back. Get rid of the idols, not just the ones made of wood and stone, but the ones lodged in your heart. Because God will not share his people's devotion with anyone.

Then God made a statement that crushed any remaining hope that someone else's righteousness could save Jerusalem. Even if Noah, Daniel, and Job were living in the city, God said, they could save only themselves. Not their sons. Not their daughters. Only themselves. The point was devastating: Jerusalem's sin had gone so far that no amount of intercession by righteous people could turn it back. The sentence had been passed.

THE USELESS VINE

Beginning in chapter 15, God shifted from direct accusations to allegories, word pictures that used familiar images to tell the truth in a way that cut deeper than a straightforward lecture.

The first was short and sharp. God asked Ezekiel a simple question: What's the wood of a grapevine good for? Can you build anything with it? Can you even make a peg to hang something on?

The answer was obvious: no. Vine wood is crooked, weak, and useless as lumber. The only value of a vine is its fruit. If a vine doesn't produce grapes, it has no purpose at all. You can't even burn it efficiently. It chars on the ends and stays soft in the middle.

That was Jerusalem. God had planted Israel as a vine and expected fruit. Instead, the vine was barren. And a fruitless vine isn't just disappointing. It's worthless. God would throw it into the fire.

THE UNFAITHFUL BRIDE

The second allegory is the longest single prophecy in the entire book of Ezekiel, and it is one of the most disturbing chapters in the Bible. Chapter 16 tells the story of Jerusalem as a woman, from birth to betrayal, and it uses language that is deliberately shocking.

God described Jerusalem's origins bluntly. The city had pagan roots, founded by Canaanites, Amorites, and Hittites. In the allegory, Jerusalem began as an abandoned newborn, thrown into a field, unwashed, with her umbilical cord still uncut. No one wanted her. No one cared whether she lived or died.

Then God passed by. He saw the baby lying in her own blood and spoke a word of life over her: "Live." He adopted her, raised her, and when she was grown, he married her. He washed her, clothed her in embroidered garments and fine leather, draped her in linen and silk, adorned her with gold and silver jewelry, and fed her the finest food. She became breathtakingly beautiful, famous among the nations. Everything she had, she received from him.

And then she took every one of those gifts and gave them away to other gods.

The language that follows is graphic and deliberately offensive. Jerusalem is compared to a woman who became a prostitute, except worse than a prostitute, because she didn't even charge for her services. She paid her lovers to come to her. She took the gold and silver God gave her and made idols. She took the food he provided and offered it to foreign gods. She even sacrificed her own children, the sons and daughters God had given her, burning them in the fires of pagan worship.

This chapter is hard to read. It's supposed to be. God wasn't trying to be tasteful. He was trying to show how his people's betrayal felt from his perspective. Imagine giving someone everything, watching them flourish because of your love, and then discovering they had taken every gift you gave them and used it to pursue someone else. That's what idolatry looks like to God. Not a minor theological error. A devastating personal betrayal.

But even chapter 16 doesn't end without hope. In the final verses, God promised that despite everything, he would remember the covenant he made in the days of Jerusalem's youth. He would establish an everlasting covenant. He would make atonement. And when he did, Jerusalem would finally be ashamed of what she had done, not because God was punishing her, but because his grace was so much greater than her sin.

THE TWO EAGLES AND THE VINE

The third allegory was a political riddle. God told Ezekiel to describe two great eagles and a vine, and then he gave the interpretation.

The first eagle, with powerful wings and colorful plumage, was Nebuchadnezzar, king of Babylon. He had come to Jerusalem (called "Lebanon" in the riddle, because of its famous cedars), plucked off the top of the cedar (King Jehoiachin), and carried him to a city of merchants (Babylon). Then the eagle planted a seed from the land in fertile soil near abundant water. This was Zedekiah, the puppet king Nebuchadnezzar installed in Jerusalem. The seed grew into a low, spreading vine. Not a towering cedar anymore, but a vine that could have thrived if it had stayed rooted where it was planted.

But then a second great eagle appeared. This was Pharaoh of Egypt. And the vine began reaching its roots and branches toward this second eagle, looking for water from a different source. Zedekiah was breaking his oath to Nebuchadnezzar and secretly making an alliance with Egypt, hoping Egypt's army would save him from Babylon.

God's verdict was severe. Zedekiah had sworn his oath of loyalty in God's name. Breaking that oath wasn't just bad politics. It was a sin against God himself. "Should he break the covenant and yet escape?" God asked. The answer was no. The vine that turned toward Egypt would be uprooted by the east wind, a common image for the hot, destructive forces that came from Babylon's direction.

But then, just when the allegory seemed to end in total destruction, God added a surprising final stanza. He himself would take a tender shoot from the top of the cedar and plant it on the high mountain of Israel. It would grow into a magnificent tree. Birds of every kind would nest in its branches and find shelter in its shade.

This was a promise of a future king from David's line. Not Zedekiah. Not Jehoiachin. Someone new. Someone God himself would plant. The image of birds finding shelter in the great tree's branches pointed to a kingdom that would welcome people from every nation.

Centuries later, Jesus would tell a parable about a tiny mustard seed that grows into a tree where the birds of the air come and nest in its branches. The echo of Ezekiel is unmistakable. The tender shoot God promised to plant would turn out to be his own Son.

WHAT THIS MEANS FOR US

First, comfortable lies are more dangerous than hard truths. The false prophets told people what they wanted to hear, and it nearly destroyed them. Surround yourself with people who will tell you the truth, even when it hurts. A friend who warns you is more valuable than a crowd that flatters you.

Second, internal idolatry is just as real as external idolatry. The elders didn't carry statues. They carried divided loyalties in their hearts. You can sit in church every Sunday and still have idols: anything you trust more than God, love more than God, or refuse to surrender to God.

Third, God takes broken promises seriously. Zedekiah's oath was made in God's name, and breaking it was an offense against God, not just against Nebuchadnezzar. Your word matters. When you make a commitment, God expects you to keep it, even when keeping it is costly.

Fourth, God's grace outlasts human failure. Even in the most horrifying chapter of the book, the allegory of the unfaithful bride, God promised an everlasting covenant and atonement. His faithfulness is not cancelled by our unfaithfulness. That doesn't make sin less serious. It makes God's love more stunning.

TALKING POINTS

1. **The false prophets told people "peace" when there was no peace.** How do you recognize the difference between someone who is telling you what you want to hear and someone who is telling you the truth? What makes it hard to listen to the truth when it's painful?

2. **God said the elders had set up "idols in their hearts."** What does internal idolatry look like for someone your age? What are the things that compete for the place in your heart that belongs to God?

3. **The allegory of the useless vine makes the point that Israel's only value was in producing fruit for God.** What kind of "fruit" do you think God is looking for in your life? What happens when we think our value comes from something other than our relationship with God?

4. **Chapter 16 tells a love story that turns into a betrayal.** Why do you think God used such an emotional, personal image to describe idolatry? How does it change your understanding of sin to think of it as breaking a relationship rather than just breaking a rule?

5. **The allegory of the two eagles ends with God planting a tender shoot that becomes a great tree.** How does this point

to Jesus? Why do you think God included this promise of hope right in the middle of so much judgment?

The lies had been exposed. The vine was burning. The bride stood condemned. The oath was broken and the east wind was coming. But on a high mountain, in soil no human hand had prepared, a tender shoot had been planted. And it would grow into something no one expected.

Turn the page.

5

YOU ARE RESPONSIBLE

The movie *October Sky* tells the true story of Homer Hickam, a teenager growing up in a coal mining town in West Virginia in the late 1950s. Everyone in Coalwood, it seemed, was destined for the same life. Your father worked the mines. His father worked the mines. And when you graduated high school, you would work the mines too. That was the deal. Nobody asked if you wanted something different. The path was set before you were born.

But Homer wanted to build rockets.

After watching Sputnik streak across the night sky, Homer became obsessed with rocketry. He and a few friends started building and launching homemade rockets in a field outside town. His father, a mine superintendent, thought it was foolish. The teachers, the neighbors, the whole town seemed to agree: you are who your father was. Where you come from determines where you end up. Your life was decided before you had any say in it.

Homer refused to accept that. And eventually, against every expectation, he won a national science fair, earned a college scholarship, and went on to become a NASA engineer. He didn't end up in the mines. His father's story was not his story.

That tension, between the life you inherited and the life you choose, is exactly what Ezekiel 18 is about. The exiles in Babylon had convinced themselves that their suffering was someone else's fault. They were paying for the sins of previous generations. Their fate had been sealed long before they were born, and there was nothing they could do about it.

God's response was blunt: that's not how this works.

SOUR GRAPES

The people had a saying. It had become so popular that Ezekiel's contemporary, the prophet Jeremiah, heard it all the way in Jerusalem: "The parents eat sour grapes, and the children's teeth are set on edge."

The meaning was simple and bitter. Our parents sinned, and we're the ones suffering for it. They ate the bad fruit, but the sour taste is in our mouths. We didn't do anything wrong. We're just stuck with the consequences of decisions that were made generations before we were born.

On the surface, this might even sound biblical. After all, the second commandment says that God "punishes the children for the sin of the parents to the third and fourth generation." And Israel's history seemed to confirm it. The northern kingdom fell because of centuries of accumulated idolatry. Jerusalem was under threat because kings like Manasseh had filled the city with abominations decades earlier. Even a Hittite king named Mursili II, who lived a thousand years before Ezekiel, had prayed to his god with an almost identical complaint:

"My father sinned, but I have not sinned. Yet the father's sin has fallen upon me."

It was a universal human instinct: blame the previous generation. And in a sense, it felt true. The exiles were in Babylon because of decisions made by kings and leaders they had never voted for. The temple was corrupted by practices that started long before most of them were born.

But there was a poison hidden inside this proverb. It turned the people into victims of fate. If your suffering was caused by your parents' sins, then repentance was pointless. Why change your behavior if your destiny was already determined by someone else's choices? The proverb didn't just explain their pain. It excused their own sin.

God shut it down. "As surely as I live," he declared, "you will no longer quote this proverb in Israel."

THREE GENERATIONS

To make his point, God told a story about three men: a father, his son, and his grandson. The father is righteous. He doesn't worship at pagan shrines. He doesn't exploit the poor. He doesn't charge interest on loans to the needy. He doesn't steal. He doesn't oppress anyone. He follows God's laws faithfully. The verdict: "He is righteous. He will surely live."

But his son is the opposite. He's violent, cruel, and idolatrous. He takes advantage of the poor, sleeps with other men's wives, and breaks every command his father kept. Does his father's righteousness protect him? No. "He will not live. Because he has done all these detestable things, he will surely die. His blood will be on his own head."

Then comes the grandson. He sees everything his father did wrong and chooses a different path. He follows God's commands, treats people justly, and refuses to repeat his father's sins. Does his father's wickedness condemn him? No. "He will not die for his father's sin. He will surely live."

The principle was revolutionary, and it cut both ways. A righteous parent cannot save a wicked child. And a wicked parent cannot condemn a righteous one. Each person stands before God on their own. Your parents' faithfulness doesn't get credited to your account, and your parents' failure doesn't get charged to it either. You are responsible for your own life.

This didn't mean that the consequences of previous generations' sins weren't real. The exiles were genuinely suffering because of decisions made before they were born. But God was drawing a line between corporate consequences (living in exile because of national sin) and personal accountability (being judged by God based on your own choices). You might not be able to control your circumstances, but you can control your response to them. And God judges the response, not the circumstance.

CAN PEOPLE REALLY CHANGE?

Then God pushed the principle even further. What about someone who has been wicked their whole life? If they genuinely turn away from their sin and start living righteously, will God hold their past against them? "None of the offenses they have committed will be remembered against them. Because of the righteous things they have done, they will live."

And the reverse: What about someone who has been righteous but then turns to evil? Will their past goodness save them? "None of the righteous things that person has done will be remembered. Because of the unfaithfulness they are guilty of, they will die."

The people didn't like this. "The Lord's way is not just!" they protested. God fired back: "Is it my way that is unjust? Is it not your ways that are unjust?"

Their complaint revealed something important. They wanted a system where past righteousness could be banked like savings, where you could store up enough good behavior to cover future failures. God said that's not how it works. What matters is the direction you're heading right now. A person moving toward God is alive, no matter how far they've come. A person moving away from God is in danger, no matter how good they used to be.

And then came one of the most beautiful verses in the book. God asked a question that exposed his own heart: "Do I take any pleasure in the death of the wicked? Rather, am I not pleased when they turn from their ways and live?"

God doesn't enjoy judgment. He isn't looking for reasons to condemn. He takes pleasure in repentance, in life, in people turning around and coming home. The whole chapter builds toward a single appeal: "Repent and live!"

A FUNERAL SONG

Chapter 19 changes the mood entirely. After the urgent plea for individual repentance, Ezekiel was told to sing a lament, a funeral song for the royal house of Judah.

The song used two images. The first was a lioness and her cubs. The lioness represented the nation, and the cubs were her kings. One young lion grew strong and learned to hunt, but he was caught in a trap and dragged away to Egypt with hooks in his jaw. This was Jehoahaz, one of Judah's last kings, who reigned for only three months before Pharaoh Necho captured him and took him to Egypt, where he died.

The lioness raised another cub. This one also grew powerful but was likewise caught in a net and taken to Babylon. This was either Jehoiachin or Zedekiah, both of whom ended their reigns in Babylonian captivity.

The second image was a vine, lush and fruitful, planted by abundant water. Its branches grew tall and visible. But it was uprooted in fury, thrown to the ground, and the east wind dried it out. Its strong branch was stripped away. Now the vine was planted in the desert, in dry and thirsty ground. Fire spread from its own branch and consumed it.

The funeral was for the dynasty of David. The royal line that had produced kings for over four hundred years was being cut down. Not by accident. Not by bad luck. By judgment. The fire that consumed the vine came from its own branch. The dynasty's destruction was self-inflicted.

Ezekiel delivered these words as a mourner, because that's what he had become ever since he swallowed the scroll of lament back in chapter 3. He wasn't gloating over Judah's fall. He was weeping over it.

THE WHOLE UGLY HISTORY

Chapter 20 is a courtroom scene. The elders of the exile came to Ezekiel again, hoping for a word from the Lord. God's answer was not what they wanted. Instead of guidance for the future, he gave them a history lesson. And it was devastating.

God told the story of Israel from the very beginning, and at every stage the story was the same.

In Egypt, before the exodus even happened, God had told the Israelites to get rid of the idols they had picked up from their Egyptian neighbors. They didn't. God was ready to pour out his wrath right there, but he held back for the sake of his own name. He had promised to rescue them, and he would not go back on his word. So he brought them out of Egypt anyway.

In the wilderness, God gave them his laws and his Sabbaths, signs of the special relationship between them. The first generation rejected those gifts. They profaned the Sabbaths and clung to their idols. God was furious but held back again, for his name's sake. He warned their children not to follow their parents' example.

The second generation did the same thing. Same rebellion. Same idolatry. Same contempt for God's commands. God held back his wrath once more, but this time he added a chilling warning: he would scatter them among the nations. Even then, he gave them over to the consequences of their own desires, letting them follow laws and practices that could only produce death, including the horrifying practice of child sacrifice.

In the promised land, the pattern continued. The people used the hills and trees God had given them as sites for idol worship. They offered sacrifices to foreign gods on the very land that was supposed to be a showcase of faithfulness.

The message was clear. The exile wasn't caused by one generation's sin. It was the culmination of a rebellion that started before Israel was even a nation. Every generation had the chance to turn back. Every generation chose not to. The exiles sitting in front of Ezekiel were not innocent victims of their grandparents' mistakes. They were the latest chapter in a very old story. And they were still doing it. Even in Babylon, even after losing everything, they were still setting up idols in their hearts.

A SHOCKING NEW EXODUS

But then, right when the history lesson seemed to end in hopeless repetition, God said something unexpected. He announced a new exodus. But this one would be different.

In the original exodus, God brought Israel out of Egypt with a mighty hand and an outstretched arm. Those words had always meant rescue. But now God used the same language and aimed it at judgment. He would gather his people from the nations, bring them into a "wilderness," and there he would confront them face to face. He would pass them under his rod, like a shepherd counting sheep, and he would separate the rebels from the faithful. The rebels would not enter the land. Only the purified remnant would come through.

This was a wilderness experience designed to do what the first wilderness experience failed to do: produce a people who actually belonged to God.

And then the chapter ended with a vision of restoration. On God's holy mountain, in the land of Israel, the people would finally serve God wholeheartedly. No more divided loyalties. No more idol worship. God would accept them like a pleasing offering. They would look back on their past and be ashamed, not because God was shaming them, but because they would finally see clearly how good he had been and how badly they had treated him.

"Then you will know that I am the Lord, when I deal with you for my name's sake, not according to your evil ways or your corrupt practices." God's restoration would not be based on Israel's merit. It would be based on his own character. He would save them not because they deserved it but because he is who he is.

WHAT THIS MEANS FOR US

First, you are not trapped by your parents' choices. Whatever mistakes your family has made, whatever patterns have been passed down, whatever dysfunction you were born into, God does not hold you responsible for someone else's sin. Your story is not finished. Your choices matter. You can break the cycle.

Second, past failure does not disqualify you from a fresh start. God promised that the sins of a person who genuinely repents will not be remembered. That's an extraordinary statement. It means the worst chapter of your life doesn't have to be the last chapter. If you're willing to turn around, God is willing to start over.

Third, past success does not guarantee future faithfulness. A person who has been walking with God for years can still walk away. Righteousness isn't a savings account you can draw from later. It's a direction you walk in every day. The question isn't "Were you faithful last year?" It's "Are you faithful now?"

Fourth, God doesn't enjoy judgment. He asked, "Do I take any pleasure in the death of the wicked?" and the answer was a resounding no. God's heart is for life, for restoration, for repentance. When he warns of consequences, it's not because he's eager to punish. It's because he's desperate for people to turn around before it's too late.

TALKING POINTS

1. **The proverb about sour grapes was a way of blaming previous generations for current suffering.** Do you ever catch yourself blaming other people for problems in your own life? What's the difference between recognizing real consequences that others caused and using blame as an excuse to avoid responsibility?

2. **God said that a wicked person who turns to righteousness will live, and their past sins won't be held against them.** How does this make you feel? Is it comforting, or does it seem unfair? Why?

3. **The people accused God of being unjust. God turned the accusation around: "Is it not your ways that are unjust?"** Why do you think people are quicker to question God's fairness than to examine their own behavior?

4. **In chapter 20, God recounted Israel's history of rebellion from Egypt through the wilderness to Canaan. At every stage he held back his wrath "for the sake of his name."** What does it mean that God acts for the sake of his name? How is that different from selfishness?

5. **God's appeal at the end of chapter 18 was simple: "Repent and live!"** Why do you think repentance is so hard? What would it look like in your own life to stop heading in one direction and start heading in another?

The history lesson was finished. The verdict was in. Every generation, from Egypt to Babylon, had chosen rebellion over faithfulness. The cycle seemed unbreakable. But God had not given up. He was planning a purification, a new wilderness where the rebels would be separated from the remnant. And for those who survived, there was a mountain waiting, a holy place where everything would finally be made right.

Turn the page.

6

THE WORST DAY

There is a scene in the movie *Bridge to Terabithia* that no one is prepared for. Jess Aarons and Leslie Burke have spent the whole story building a friendship, creating an imaginary kingdom in the woods behind their homes, finding in each other the kind of connection that makes the rest of the world bearable. Leslie is brave and creative and full of life. She's the best thing that has happened to Jess in a long time.

And then, without warning, she's gone. Leslie dies in an accident while Jess is away on a field trip. He comes home to find his family silent, his father waiting with the news. And Jess doesn't believe it. He can't. The world continues spinning around him, but everything has changed in a single moment. The rest of the movie is about Jess learning how to carry a grief that feels too heavy for his body to hold.

That scene came to mind when I read Ezekiel 24. Because in the middle of the most devastating section of the entire book, in the middle of oracles about swords and siege and slaughter, God turns to his prophet and says something that stops everything cold.

"Son of man, with one blow I am about to take away from you the delight of your eyes."

Ezekiel's wife was about to die. And God told him he was not allowed to mourn.

We'll get there. But first, we need to walk through the chapters that lead up to that moment, because they build toward it with a terrible, mounting pressure. Ezekiel 21–24 is the darkest stretch in the entire book. The sword is drawn. The city is indicted. The sisters are condemned. The pot boils over. And then, at the very end, the prophet's own heart is broken. This is what it looks like when judgment stops being a threat and becomes a reality.

THE DRAWN SWORD

Chapter 21 opens with an image that would have made every listener's blood run cold. God told Ezekiel: "I am about to draw my sword from its sheath and cut off from you both the righteous and the wicked."

A drawn sword. Not sheathed. Not hanging on the wall as a warning. Drawn, polished, sharpened, ready for slaughter. God described it with the intensity of a weapon being prepared for battle: "sharpened for the kill, polished to flash like lightning." The repetition was deliberate. God wanted the people to feel the weight of what was coming. This was not a distant threat. The blade was out.

Then the chapter shifted to a scene that would have been chillingly familiar to anyone living in the ancient world. God told Ezekiel to draw a map in the dirt, marking a road that split into two paths. One path led to Rabbah, the capital of Ammon.

The other led to Jerusalem. Standing at the crossroads was the king of Babylon, Nebuchadnezzar, deciding which city to attack first.

To make his decision, Nebuchadnezzar used divination. He shook labeled arrows in a quiver and drew one out. He consulted his household idols. He examined the liver of a slaughtered sheep, reading the patterns on its surface the way Babylonian priests were trained to do. These were standard methods of seeking guidance from the gods in the ancient world. Archaeologists have found clay models of sheep livers in Mesopotamia, used as training tools for priests learning to read the omens.

The lot fell on Jerusalem.

Here's the irony that Ezekiel's audience needed to grasp. Nebuchadnezzar thought his gods were guiding him. But it was the Lord who was directing the Babylonian king's hand. The pagan divination methods were producing the result that God had already determined. The most powerful army in the world was a tool in the hand of Israel's God, aimed directly at his own city.

Then came a word for Zedekiah, the last king of Judah, called here "the wicked prince of Israel." God told him to remove his turban and his crown. The symbols of royal authority were being stripped away. "It will not be restored," God said, "until he comes to whom it rightfully belongs." The throne of David was being emptied. But the language pointed forward. Someday, someone would come who had the right to wear that crown. The line of David was interrupted, not erased.

A CITY FULL OF BLOOD

Chapter 22 is a courtroom scene where the judge reads a list of charges against the defendant, and the list goes on and on.

God called Jerusalem "the city of bloodshed" and then laid out the evidence. The crimes touched every level of society. The leaders used their power to shed blood and enrich themselves. People treated their parents with contempt. Foreigners were exploited. Orphans and widows were mistreated. The priests blurred the line between what was holy and what was common, and they ignored the Sabbath. People accepted bribes, charged interest on loans to the poor, and used slander to destroy their neighbors. Sexual boundaries were violated. The list covered ceremonial laws, moral laws, and social justice, all broken, all at once, all throughout the city.

God compared the people to dross, the worthless residue left over when metal is refined in a furnace. When a metalworker melts down silver, the impurities float to the surface and get skimmed off. That's what the people of Jerusalem had become. They were not the silver. They were the scum.

So God declared that he would gather them into Jerusalem like metal into a furnace and melt them with the fire of his anger. The siege itself would be the furnace, and the heat would be God's wrath.

The chapter ended with a devastating search. God said: "I looked for someone among them who would build up the wall and stand before me in the gap on behalf of the land so I would not have to destroy it, but I found no one."

God had been looking for an intercessor, someone who would stand between his wrath and the city, someone who would pray, who would lead, who would call the people back. But every leader had failed. The kings were predators. The priests were negligent. The prophets were liars. The officials were corrupt. The people of the land exploited anyone weaker than themselves. No one stood in the gap. And so the judgment fell.

TWO SISTERS

Chapter 23 told one more allegory, the last in a series that had been building since chapter 16. This time the story was about two sisters named Oholah and Oholibah. Oholah represented Samaria, the capital of the northern kingdom. Oholibah represented Jerusalem.

Both sisters were unfaithful. Both pursued political alliances with foreign nations instead of trusting God. Ezekiel described their behavior using the same graphic language of adultery and prostitution that appeared in chapter 16. The point was the same: Israel's political alliances were acts of spiritual betrayal. Every time the nation turned to Egypt, Assyria, or Babylon for help instead of turning to God, it was like a wife running to another man.

Oholah, the older sister, had chased after Assyria. She admired their soldiers, their uniforms, their power. So God handed her over to the very nation she desired. Assyria conquered Samaria in 722 BC, stripped her bare, and destroyed her.

You'd think Oholibah would have learned from her sister's fate. She didn't. She did the same thing, only worse. She pursued Assyria, then Babylon, then went crawling back to Egypt. Her desire for foreign alliances was insatiable. She was so consumed with political maneuvering that she forgot the God who had loved her, provided for her, and given her everything she had.

God's sentence was familiar by now: her lovers would become her punishers. The nations she had chased would turn against her, strip her of everything, and leave her exposed. She would drink the same cup of wrath that her sister had drunk.

The allegory was crude, blunt, and intentionally offensive. God wanted the exiles to feel the ugliness of what their nation had done. Political unfaithfulness wasn't a strategic miscalculation. It was adultery against a faithful husband. And the consequences were about to arrive.

THE RUSTY POT

Then came the day everything changed. Chapter 24 opens with a date that would be remembered forever: the tenth day of the tenth month of the ninth year of Zedekiah's reign. In our calendar, that's January 15, 588 BC. On that day, hundreds of miles away in Jerusalem, Nebuchadnezzar's army arrived at the city walls and began the siege.

Ezekiel was in Babylon. He had no messenger, no news report, no way of knowing what was happening in Jerusalem. But God told him. "Son of man, record this date, this very date, because the king of Babylon has laid siege to Jerusalem this very day."

Then God gave Ezekiel a parable to perform. He was to put a cooking pot on the fire, fill it with water and the choicest cuts of meat, and bring it to a boil. The pot represented Jerusalem. The meat represented the people inside. They had believed they were the "choice pieces" God had protected by keeping them in the city while others were exiled. They thought the pot was keeping them safe.

But this pot was rusted. Its sides were encrusted with buildup that no amount of scrubbing could remove. The rust represented the bloodshed and corruption that had saturated the city so thoroughly that it could never be cleaned. God's solution was to empty the pot completely, piece by piece, and then set the empty pot back on the fire until the rust itself burned away.

The message was devastating: Jerusalem was beyond cleaning. The only solution was to empty it of people and burn it until there was nothing left but bare metal. The siege would not end in rescue. It would end in destruction.

THE DELIGHT OF HIS EYES

And then God said something that no amount of theological preparation could have softened. "Son of man, with one blow I am about to take away from you the delight of your eyes. Yet do not lament or weep or shed any tears. Groan quietly; do not mourn for the dead. Keep your turban fastened and your sandals on your feet. Do not cover your mustache and beard, and do not eat the customary food of mourners."

God was telling Ezekiel that his wife was going to die. Today. Suddenly. And he was not allowed to grieve publicly.

In the ancient world, mourning was not a private affair. When someone you loved died, the whole community participated. You tore your clothes. You took off your shoes. You covered part of your face. You sat on the ground. Friends brought you food. The rituals were visible, physical, and communal. They gave grief a shape and a container.

God told Ezekiel to skip all of it. No torn clothes. No bare feet. No covered face. No mourning food. He could groan quietly, but that was it. He was to carry the most devastating loss of his life in near-total silence.

That evening, Ezekiel spoke to the people. The next morning, his wife was dead.

He did exactly what God had told him to do. He did not mourn.

The people noticed. Of course they noticed. A man whose wife has just died, standing there in his turban and sandals, dry-eyed and silent? It was shocking. They came to him and asked: "Won't you tell us what these things have to do with us? Why are you acting this way?"

And Ezekiel answered with the message God had given him. "The delight of your eyes," he said, meaning the temple, was about to be struck down. Their sons and daughters left behind in Jerusalem would fall by the sword. And when that happened, they would do exactly what Ezekiel was doing. They would not mourn publicly. Not because they wouldn't want to, but because the grief would be too enormous, too total, too paralyzing for the normal rituals to contain. They would waste away under the weight of their sins, groaning inwardly, unable to process what they had lost.

Ezekiel's silent grief was the final sign-act. His body had been a sermon throughout his ministry. He had lain on his side, starved himself, shaved his head, dug through walls, and packed exile bags. Now his body preached its most painful message yet: this is what it will feel like when everything you love is taken away.

God added one more promise. On the day a fugitive arrived from Jerusalem with the news that the city had fallen, Ezekiel's mouth would be opened. His years of restricted speech would end. He would speak freely again. The mourning period that had defined his entire ministry would finally be over.

But that day was still years away. For now, the prophet stood in silence beside the body of the woman he loved, waiting for a word from a city that was already burning.

WHAT THIS MEANS FOR US

First, God's patience has a final limit. For chapters now, we have watched the warnings pile up. Sign-acts, allegories, history lessons, indictments. God sent everything short of the judgment itself. But when the tenth day of the tenth month arrived, the waiting was over. Patience is not the same as passivity. God gives time to repent, but he does not give forever.

Second, leadership failure has devastating consequences. God searched for someone to stand in the gap and found no one. Every level of leadership in Jerusalem had failed. This is a sobering reminder that the people we trust to lead, whether in government, in churches, or in families, carry real responsibility. When leaders fail, the people under their care suffer.

Third, God asks the hardest things of the people closest to him. Ezekiel wasn't punished by losing his wife. God called her the "delight of your eyes" with tenderness. But God asked his prophet to bear something unbearable, because Ezekiel's silent grief would become the most powerful sermon he ever preached. Sometimes the people God uses most are the ones he asks to carry the heaviest weight.

Fourth, grief is real, and God does not minimize it. The fact that God told Ezekiel to suppress his mourning didn't mean grief was unimportant. It meant that something unprecedented was about to happen, something so far beyond normal loss that normal mourning wouldn't fit. God acknowledged the pain. He called Ezekiel's wife the delight of his eyes. He knew what he was asking.

TALKING POINTS

1. **Nebuchadnezzar used pagan divination methods to decide where to attack, but God was the one directing the outcome.** What does this tell you about God's control over events, even when the people involved don't know he's at work? How does this change the way you think about things that seem random or out of control?

2. **God said, "I looked for someone to stand in the gap, but found no one."** What does it mean to "stand in the gap" for others? How can an ordinary person, even a kid, make a difference when the people around them are making bad choices?

3. **The two sisters in chapter 23 kept pursuing alliances with foreign nations instead of trusting God.** What are some things people your age are tempted to rely on for security or identity instead of trusting God? Why is it so hard to let God be enough?

4. **God told Ezekiel not to mourn his wife's death publicly.** How do you think that felt? Why would God ask something so painful of someone he loved? Have you ever had to do

something incredibly hard because you knew it mattered for someone other than yourself?

5. **Ezekiel's silent grief was the most powerful sign-act in the book.** Why do you think silence can sometimes communicate more than words? When have you seen someone's quiet endurance speak louder than anything they could have said?

The pot was empty. The wife was buried without a funeral. The sword was drawn and would not return to its sheath until the work was done.

Ezekiel's ministry to his own nation was finished. When he spoke again, the world would be different. Jerusalem would be gone. The temple would be ash. And the prophet would turn his gaze outward, toward the nations that had watched Israel's destruction and laughed. They were about to discover that the God of Israel had not lost his power. He had only been using it on his own people first.

Turn the page.

7

AGAINST THE NATIONS

Two hundred and fifty years after Ezekiel wrote his prophecies against the city of Tyre, a young military commander named Alexander the Great stood on the Mediterranean coast and stared at the problem in front of him.

Tyre was an island. The main city sat about half a mile offshore, surrounded by deep water and massive walls that rose directly from the sea. For centuries, this had made Tyre virtually unconquerable. Armies could destroy the mainland settlements, but the island city simply watched from the water, safe and smug. Nebuchadnezzar himself had besieged Tyre for thirteen years and never fully took it.

Alexander was not Nebuchadnezzar. When the Tyrians refused to surrender, Alexander did something no one had attempted before. He ordered his engineers to build a causeway straight out into the sea, using the rubble and stone from the destroyed mainland city as fill. His soldiers literally scraped the old city bare, down to the bedrock, and dumped it into the water. It took months. The Tyrians attacked from ships, set fire to the construction, killed workers by the hundreds. But

Alexander kept building. When the causeway finally reached the island, his army stormed the walls and conquered the city.

Today, if you visit the site of ancient Tyre in modern Lebanon, you can still see the remnants of that causeway. The island is no longer an island. Sand and sediment have built up around Alexander's land bridge over the centuries, permanently connecting it to the shore. And the ancient mainland city? It's gone. Scraped clean. A bare rock where local fishermen spread their nets to dry.

Ezekiel had written: "They will break down your walls and demolish your fine houses and throw your stones, timber and rubble into the sea. I will make you a bare rock, and you will become a place to spread fishnets."

He wrote that in approximately 586 BC. Alexander fulfilled it in 332 BC. Ezekiel never saw it happen. But the God who gave him the words knew exactly what was coming.

WHY THESE CHAPTERS EXIST

After the death of Ezekiel's wife and the beginning of the siege of Jerusalem in chapter 24, you might expect the book to jump straight to the news of the city's fall. It doesn't. Instead, Ezekiel turns his attention outward, away from Israel, toward the surrounding nations. Chapters 25–32 contain prophecies against seven foreign powers: Ammon, Moab, Edom, Philistia, Tyre, Sidon, and Egypt.

Why here? Why now?

Because God's judgment doesn't stop at Israel's borders. The nations that watched Jerusalem burn and celebrated, the empires that exploited Israel's weakness, the kings who thought they were untouchable, all of them would answer to the same God who had judged his own people. If God was willing to destroy his own temple and exile his own nation because of their sin, the surrounding nations had no reason to think they were safe.

But there's a deeper reason these prophecies are placed here. Ezekiel's audience was in mourning. They had lost their city, their temple, and their identity. They needed to hear that the nations mocking them would not have the last laugh. Before the book turns to the hope of restoration in later chapters, God first deals with Israel's enemies. Comfort comes, but only after the bullies face their own reckoning.

THE NEIGHBORS WHO LAUGHED

Chapter 25 moves quickly through Israel's four closest neighbors, starting to the northeast and sweeping clockwise.

Ammon had clapped its hands and stamped its feet in glee when Jerusalem fell. "Aha!" they shouted over the ruined temple. God's response was swift: the people of the East would overrun Ammon. Their capital, Rabbah, would become a pasture for camels. They had treated Israel's tragedy as entertainment. Now they would become a spectacle themselves.

Moab, to the east, had drawn a particular conclusion from Jerusalem's destruction: "Look, the house of Judah has become like all the other nations." In other words, Israel's God was no different from any other god. He couldn't protect his people. Moab insulted not just Israel but the Lord himself. For that, Moab's defenses would be stripped away and its cities exposed to invaders.

Edom, to the south, had done something worse than mock. Edom had taken revenge. When Jerusalem fell and refugees tried to flee south, the Edomites, who were related to Israel through Esau, attacked the fleeing survivors instead of helping them. They turned on their own family in the worst possible moment. God promised to stretch out his hand against Edom and cut off both man and beast.

Philistia, to the west, had acted with ancient, deep-seated malice. Their hostility toward Israel stretched back centuries, to the time of the judges and King David. They took advantage of Judah's weakness to settle old scores. God's vengeance would come upon them with furious rebukes.

The pattern was consistent. Each nation's crime was specific: gloating, insulting God, attacking refugees, or exploiting weakness. And each nation's punishment was tailored to fit. God noticed exactly how each one had treated his people in their darkest hour.

THE SHIP THAT SANK

The prophecy against Tyre is the longest of the group (chapters 26–28), and it's one of the most vivid sections in the entire book.

Tyre was no ordinary city. It was the economic superpower of the ancient Mediterranean, a Phoenician port city that had built a commercial empire stretching from Spain to Persia. Tyrian ships carried goods across the known world: cedar from Lebanon, silver from Spain, horses from Turkey, spices from Arabia, linen from Egypt, ivory and ebony from Africa. The list of Tyre's trading partners in chapter 27 reads like an atlas of the ancient world. Every luxury, every rare commodity, every exotic material passed through Tyre's harbors.

The city was also proud beyond measure. Its island location made it feel invincible. When Jerusalem fell, Tyre's response was purely commercial: "Aha! The gate to the nations is broken, and its doors have swung open to me. Now that she lies in ruins I will prosper." Tyre didn't mourn Jerusalem. It saw a business opportunity. With Jerusalem gone, trade routes would shift, and Tyre would profit from the chaos.

God's response filled three chapters.

First, in chapter 26, God announced that many nations would come against Tyre like waves crashing against a shore. Nebuchadnezzar would besiege the mainland settlements with full military force: siege walls, ramps, battering rams, cavalry, and chariots. The city's walls would be broken, its towers pulled down, and the rubble scraped into the sea until nothing remained but bare rock, a place for fishermen to spread their nets.

Then, in chapter 27, Ezekiel composed one of the most remarkable poems in the Bible: a lament for Tyre portrayed as a magnificent ship. The city was described as a vessel built from the finest materials in the world. Its planks were juniper from Mount Hermon. Its mast was cedar from Lebanon. Its oars were oak from Bashan. Its deck was inlaid with ivory from Cyprus. Its sail was embroidered Egyptian linen. Its crew came from the best Phoenician cities. Its soldiers were mercenaries from Persia, North Africa, and Turkey.

The ship was loaded with cargo from every corner of the known world. It was the pride of the seas, stunning and unstoppable.

And then an east wind hit it. In one verse, the poem shifted from glory to disaster: "The east wind has broken you to pieces in the heart of the seas." The east wind in Ezekiel always represented Babylon, the destructive force that God sent from the east. The great ship, heavy with cargo and pride, broke apart and sank. Its cargo, its crew, its wealth, its reputation, all of it went to the bottom of the sea. The sailors on shore wailed, threw dust on their heads, and mourned: "Who was ever silenced like Tyre, surrounded by the sea?"

Finally, in chapter 28, the prophecy narrowed its focus to the king of Tyre himself. And here the language became extraordinary.

The king had said in his heart, "I am a god. I sit on the throne of a god in the heart of the seas." He wasn't just proud. He had convinced himself he was divine. His wisdom had built a commercial empire. His wealth was beyond imagination. And success had inflated his self-image until he believed he was more than human.

God's response used imagery borrowed from the Garden of Eden. The king was described as a figure who had been in Eden, adorned with every precious stone, walking on the holy mountain of God among stones of fire. He was created beautiful and blameless. But his heart became proud because of his splendor, and his wisdom was corrupted by his brilliance. So God cast him to the ground and made a spectacle of him before kings.

Scholars have debated for centuries whether this passage is only about the human king of Tyre or whether it also echoes a larger story about the fall of a heavenly being. What's clear is the point Ezekiel was making: pride that claims to be divine always ends in destruction. The king who said "I am a god" would die like any other man. The economic empire that seemed eternal would sink like a ship in a storm.

THE MONSTER IN THE NILE

The prophecy against Egypt is even longer than the one against Tyre, spanning four full chapters (29–32) and containing seven separate oracles delivered over a period of roughly sixteen years.

Egypt held a special place in Israel's story. It was the land of slavery, the place God had rescued his people from in the most dramatic event in the Old Testament. But it was also the nation Israel kept running back to for help. Every time Judah faced a crisis, instead of trusting God, they sent messengers to Pharaoh begging for military support. Egypt was the "other lover" in Ezekiel's earlier allegories, the foreign power Jerusalem kept pursuing instead of depending on the Lord.

And Egypt always let them down. When Nebuchadnezzar besieged Jerusalem, Pharaoh Hophra sent an army to help, but the Babylonians quickly drove it back. Egypt's support was like leaning on a staff made of reed. It looked sturdy, but when you put your weight on it, it snapped and stabbed you in the hand.

God described Pharaoh as a great monster lounging in the Nile, boasting, "The Nile belongs to me. I made it for myself." The image was probably that of a crocodile, the most feared creature in Egypt's waters. But God would put hooks in the monster's jaws, drag it out of the river, and leave it in the desert for the birds and beasts to devour.

Egypt would be desolated for forty years, a period that echoed Israel's own forty years of wilderness wandering. Egyptians would be scattered among the nations. And when they returned, they would be a shadow of their former selves, a lowly kingdom that would never again rule the nations.

In chapter 31, God compared Egypt to Assyria, the empire that had dominated the world just decades earlier. Assyria had been like a magnificent cedar tree, taller and more beautiful than any tree in the forest. Its branches sheltered nations. Its roots drank from deep waters. But it grew proud, and God handed it over to a foreign power. The great cedar was cut down. Its branches lay broken on every hillside. The nations that had sheltered in its shade moved on.

The lesson was impossible to miss: if Assyria, with all its power, could be felled like a tree, what made Egypt think it was safe?

The final chapter of this section, chapter 32, described Pharaoh's descent into the realm of the dead. There, in the pit, Egypt would find itself in the company of other fallen empires: Assyria, Elam, Meshek, Tubal, Edom, and the princes of the north. All of them had once been fearsome. All of them had terrified the living. Now they lay together in the grave, stripped of their power, their weapons beside them, their glory gone.

It was a grim and haunting image. The graveyard of empires, all of them laid low by the God who controls the rise and fall of every nation on earth.

WHAT THIS MEANS FOR US

First, God holds all nations accountable, not just his own people. The surrounding nations didn't have the covenant.

They didn't have the law or the prophets. But they were still responsible for how they treated others, especially the vulnerable. You don't need a Bible to know that gloating over someone's suffering is wrong. God's moral standards apply to everyone.

Second, pride is the most dangerous sin of all. The king of Tyre thought he was a god. Pharaoh claimed to have created the Nile. Both were brought low. Pride convinces you that your success is entirely your own doing, that you don't need anyone, and that you're untouchable. God's response to that kind of pride is always the same: the one who exalts himself will be humbled.

Third, the empires that look invincible are always temporary. Assyria fell. Tyre fell. Egypt fell. Babylon itself would eventually fall. Every superpower in human history has eventually crumbled. The only kingdom that lasts forever is God's. If you're tempted to put your ultimate trust in a nation, an institution, or any human power structure, these chapters are a reminder that none of them will stand forever.

Fourth, how you treat people in their worst moments reveals who you really are. Ammon clapped. Moab mocked. Edom attacked refugees. Tyre calculated profits. God noticed all of it. The way you respond when someone else is suffering says more about your character than anything you do when life is easy.

TALKING POINTS

1. **Each of Israel's neighbors responded differently to Jerusalem's destruction: gloating, mocking, attacking, or profiting.** Which of those responses do you think is the worst,

and why? Have you ever seen someone treated badly when they were already down?

2. **The king of Tyre said, "I am a god." That sounds extreme, but pride takes subtler forms too.** What does pride look like in the life of someone your age? How can success or talent make people forget that everything they have ultimately comes from God?

3. **Tyre is described as a beautiful, powerful ship that sinks in a storm.** Why do you think Ezekiel used a ship as the metaphor? What does it say about the relationship between wealth, beauty, and vulnerability?

4. **God compared Egypt to Assyria, the great cedar that was cut down.** Why do you think God used a recent historical example (Assyria had fallen only about twenty years earlier) to make his point? How can looking at history help us avoid the same mistakes?

5. **Chapter 32 pictures fallen empires lying together in the grave, all of them equally powerless.** What does this image teach you about the difference between earthly power and the kind of power that actually lasts?

The nations had been warned. The bullies had been named. The empires that thought they were gods had been sentenced to the grave. Tyre would become a bare rock. Egypt would shrink to a shadow. The proud would be humbled, and the God of Israel would be recognized not just by his own people but by every nation on earth.

Now the book could turn. The judgment was nearly complete. Somewhere in Babylon, a fugitive was making his way toward Ezekiel with the news everyone had been dreading: Jerusalem had fallen. And when that word arrived, everything would change. The prophet's mouth would open. The mourning would end. And for the first time in this dark, devastating book, hope would begin to rise.

Turn the page.

8

THE WATCHMAN AND THE SHEPHERD

Picture the worst coach you can imagine. Not a coach who's tough on you because they want you to get better. That kind of coach can be hard to deal with, but deep down you know they care.

No, picture a coach who doesn't care about the team at all. They show up late. They play favorites. The strongest players get all the attention and the best positions while the weaker ones get ignored or shoved aside. When someone gets hurt, the coach barely looks up. When the team loses, it's always the players' fault, never the coaching.

And the worst part? The coach uses the team's resources for personal benefit, taking the best equipment, using the team's budget for personal trips, feeding their own reputation while the players go without.

Now imagine that every coach, every captain, every leader in your entire league behaved that way. Not one of them cared about the players. Not one of them used their position to serve anyone but themselves. The strong players bullied the weak ones, and nobody in charge lifted a finger. Kids got pushed out of the sport entirely, wandering off with no one coming to look for them.

That's the picture God painted in Ezekiel 34 when he described the leaders of Israel as shepherds. And his response was unlike anything the people expected. He didn't just promise to send better shepherds. He said he would come and do the job himself.

THE WATCHMAN RETURNS

Chapter 33 marks one of the most important turning points in the entire book. Everything before this chapter was about judgment. Everything after it begins turning toward hope. And the chapter opens by taking Ezekiel back to where he started.

God recommissioned Ezekiel as a watchman.

We first heard this language back in chapter 3, when God originally gave Ezekiel his role. A watchman in the ancient world was a sentry posted on the city wall, responsible for scanning the horizon and sounding the alarm when danger approached. If the watchman blew the trumpet and the people ignored it, their deaths were their own responsibility. But if the watchman saw the enemy coming and stayed silent, God would hold the watchman accountable for every life lost.

Now, in chapter 33, God expanded and formalized that role. The principle was the same: Ezekiel was responsible for delivering the warning, not for making people listen. But God added something he hadn't emphasized as strongly the first time. He paused the indictment to make a statement about his own heart that changes the tone of everything that follows.

"As surely as I live," God declared, "I take no pleasure in the death of the wicked, but rather that they turn from their ways and live. Turn! Turn from your evil ways! Why will you die, house of Israel?"

This wasn't a cold judge handing down a sentence. This was a father pleading with his children to come home. God didn't want Israel to die. He never had. Every warning, every sign-act, every devastating oracle had been an attempt to provoke repentance, not to punish for the sake of punishing. Even now, after years of rebellion, after the siege had already begun, God was still saying: turn around. It's not too late. I want you to live.

The chapter then revisited the principles of individual responsibility from chapter 18. A righteous person who turns to evil will die. A wicked person who turns to righteousness will live. God judges people by the direction they're heading, not by the direction they came from. The past doesn't lock you in. What matters is what you do next.

THE CITY HAS FALLEN

Then came the moment the entire book had been building toward. A fugitive arrived from Jerusalem. He had traveled roughly 900 miles from the ruined city to the exiles in Babylon, carrying the worst news imaginable: "The city has fallen."

It was January of 585 BC, about a year and a half after Nebuchadnezzar's army had breached the walls. The delay was simply the time it took for someone to make the long, dangerous journey on foot from Palestine to Mesopotamia. But for the exiles who had been waiting, hoping against hope that somehow the city would survive, those words hit like a physical blow. Jerusalem was gone. The temple was destroyed. The dream was over.

The night before the fugitive arrived, something happened to Ezekiel. God opened his mouth. Since the day his wife had died and the siege began, Ezekiel had been living under the restriction God had placed on him years earlier. He could only speak when God gave him a specific message to deliver. The rest of the time, silence.

Now the silence was over. When the fugitive arrived the next morning with his devastating report, Ezekiel could speak freely for the first time in years. His prophetic ministry entered a new phase. The warnings had been vindicated. The judgment had fallen. Now it was time for something different.

But before the hope could begin, God had two more hard truths to deliver.

First, the people still living in the ruins of Jerusalem had convinced themselves that because Abraham was one man and inherited the whole land, they, as survivors, had an even greater claim to it. God demolished that logic. Abraham had obeyed. These survivors were still eating meat with the blood in it, worshiping idols, and shedding innocent blood. The land wasn't theirs by right. More judgment was coming for those who remained.

Second, the exiles sitting around Ezekiel had a problem of their own. God told the prophet something both flattering and devastating: "Your people talk about you beside the walls and at the doors of their houses. They say to each other, 'Come and hear the message from the Lord.' They come to you as people usually do, and they sit before you and hear your words, but they do not put them into practice."

The exiles loved listening to Ezekiel. He was like a singer with a beautiful voice performing lovely songs. They enjoyed the experience. They were entertained. But they didn't change their behavior. They heard the words and walked away unchanged.

God's assessment was blunt: "When all this comes true, and it surely will, then they will know that a prophet has been among them." The proof of Ezekiel's authenticity would come not from the audience's response but from the fulfillment of his words. Whether they listened or not, the truth was the truth.

WOE TO THE SHEPHERDS

Chapter 34 is one of the most beloved and important chapters in the entire book. It opens with the harshest indictment of Israel's leaders found anywhere in the prophets, and it ends with one of the most tender promises in the Old Testament.

God told Ezekiel to prophesy against the shepherds of Israel. In the ancient Near East, calling a king a "shepherd" was standard language. From the earliest Sumerian kings to the great rulers of Babylon and Assyria, monarchs described themselves as shepherds of their people. The title carried specific expectations: a shepherd protects the flock, feeds them, leads them to good pasture, binds up the injured, searches for the lost, and defends them from predators. A good shepherd puts the flock's needs above his own.

Israel's shepherds had done the opposite. "You eat the curds, clothe yourselves with the wool, and slaughter the choice animals, but you do not take care of the flock. You have not strengthened the weak or healed the sick or bound up the injured. You have not brought back the strays or searched for the lost. You have ruled them harshly and brutally."

The charge list was devastating. Every single responsibility of a shepherd had been neglected or reversed. Instead of feeding the flock, the leaders fed themselves. Instead of healing the sick, they ignored them. Instead of searching for the lost, they let them wander. Instead of protecting the weak, they ruled with cruelty. The sheep had been scattered across the face of the earth because there was no real shepherd caring for them. They had become food for every wild animal, prey for every predator, and no one went looking for them.

God's anger burned against these leaders: "I am against the shepherds, and I will hold them accountable for my flock. I will remove them from tending the flock so that the shepherds can no longer feed themselves."

The leaders were fired. Their job was over. They had failed, and God was done giving them chances.

GOD WILL SEARCH FOR HIS SHEEP

But the story didn't end with judgment on the leaders. What came next is one of the most stunning reversals in all of Scripture.

"For this is what the Sovereign Lord says: I myself will search for my sheep and look after them. As a shepherd looks after his scattered flock when he is with them, I myself will tend my sheep and have them lie down. I will search for the lost and bring back the strays. I will bind up the injured and strengthen the weak."

God didn't announce that he would hire better shepherds. He didn't say he would reform the system or train new leaders. He said *I myself*. God would personally take over the role that every human leader had failed to fill. He would do the searching. He would do the healing. He would do the feeding and protecting and gathering.

Think about what that meant for the exiles hearing these words. They had been scattered by bad leadership, failed by every king and priest and prophet who was supposed to care for them. They were sitting in Babylon, far from home, convinced that God himself had abandoned them along with everyone else.

And God said: I am coming to find you. Personally.

He promised to gather them from all the places where they had been scattered. He would bring them back to their own land, to the mountains of Israel, and feed them in good pasture. He would make them lie down in safety, no longer afraid of predators, no longer at the mercy of leaders who didn't care.

But God wasn't just gentle. He also promised to judge within the flock itself. Not all the sheep were innocent victims. Some of the stronger sheep had been shoving the weaker ones aside, trampling the pasture so others couldn't eat, muddying the water so others couldn't drink. God would judge between the fat sheep and the lean sheep, between the bullies and the bullied. Justice would come not just for the leaders but within the community itself.

ONE SHEPHERD

Then God made a promise that pointed far beyond the immediate future. "I will place over them one shepherd, my servant David, and he will tend them. He will tend them and be their shepherd. I the Lord will be their God, and my servant David will be prince among them."

This wasn't a promise to resurrect the historical King David, who had been dead for over four hundred years. It was a promise of a future king from David's line, a ruler who would finally be the shepherd Israel had always needed. A king who would actually feed the flock, actually care for the weak, actually search for the lost.

Every king in David's dynasty had been measured against this standard, and every one had fallen short. Some, like Josiah, had come close. Most hadn't even tried. But God was promising that one day, a descendant of David would come who would get it right. One shepherd. Not a succession of failures. One.

The earliest Christians recognized this promise immediately. When Jesus said, "I am the good shepherd. The good shepherd lays down his life for the sheep," he was claiming to be the fulfillment of Ezekiel 34. When he told the parable of the shepherd who leaves ninety-nine sheep to search for the one that was lost, he was acting out what God had promised through Ezekiel: "I myself will search for my sheep."

Jesus didn't just come to teach people about God. He came to be the shepherd God had promised to send, the one who would do what every human leader had failed to do. He fed the hungry. He healed the sick. He searched for the lost. He bound up the broken. And he laid down his life for the flock.

THE COVENANT OF PEACE

The chapter ended with a promise that stretched beyond anything the exiles could have imagined. "I will make a covenant of peace with them and rid the land of savage beasts so that they may live in the wilderness and sleep in the forests in safety. I will make them and the places surrounding my hill a blessing. I will send down showers in season; there will be showers of blessing."

A covenant of peace. Not just the absence of war. A deep, complete restoration of everything that had been broken. The land would produce abundantly. The trees would bear fruit. The people would be secure. No more slavery. No more fear. No more shame among the nations.

"Then they will know that I, the Lord their God, am with them and that they, the Israelites, are my people," declares the Sovereign Lord. "You are my sheep, the sheep of my pasture, and I am your God."

After chapters of judgment, after the sword and the siege and the scattered flock and the failed leaders and the fallen city, God's final word in this section was breathtakingly simple: You are mine. I am yours. And I am not letting go.

WHAT THIS MEANS FOR US

First, God's heart is for life, not death. "Why will you die?" he pleaded. Even after everything Israel had done, God was still calling them to repentance, still offering a way back. If you think you've gone too far for God to want you, Ezekiel 33:11 says otherwise. He takes no pleasure in your destruction. He wants you to turn around and live.

Second, hearing God's word without obeying it is worthless. The exiles loved listening to Ezekiel the way you might enjoy a good podcast or a moving song. But enjoyment isn't obedience. If God's word doesn't change how you live, you haven't really heard it. You've just been entertained.

Third, God holds leaders accountable. The shepherds of Israel weren't punished because they were incompetent. They were punished because they were selfish. They used their position to serve themselves instead of the people in their care. Anyone in a position of influence, whether that's a minister, a parent, a teacher, a team captain, or a student leader, will answer to God for how they treated the people who depended on them.

Fourth, when every human leader fails, God steps in personally. The promise of Ezekiel 34 isn't just that better leaders are coming. It's that God himself will shepherd his people. And he fulfilled that promise in Jesus, the Good Shepherd who searches for the lost, heals the broken, and lays down his life for the sheep.

TALKING POINTS

1. **God said he takes no pleasure in the death of the wicked.** How does that statement change the way you understand God's judgment throughout the book of Ezekiel? Does it surprise you? Why or why not?

2. **The exiles enjoyed listening to Ezekiel but didn't put his words into practice.** How do you recognize the difference in your own life between genuinely hearing God's word and just enjoying the experience of being around it?

3. **God's indictment of the shepherds listed specific failures: not strengthening the weak, not healing the sick, not searching for the lost, ruling harshly.** If you were in a leadership role (captain, older sibling, group leader), which of these failures would be the easiest to fall into? Why?

4. God said "I myself" would search for his sheep. Why do you think God chose to do this personally instead of simply appointing better leaders? What does this tell you about his character?

5. Jesus said, "I am the good shepherd." How do you see Jesus fulfilling the specific promises of Ezekiel 34? What does it mean for your life to know that the Good Shepherd is actively looking for lost and hurting sheep?

The watchman had been recommissioned. The city had fallen. The bad shepherds had been condemned. And in their place, God had made a promise: he himself would come, search for his scattered sheep, and place over them one shepherd, his servant David, who would tend them with the care they had never known.

But the promise didn't stop there. In the next chapters, God would show Ezekiel something that made even this seem small. He would take him to a valley full of bones, ask the most impossible question in the Bible, and reveal a future so stunning that the prophet could barely believe what he was seeing.

Turn the page.

9

THE VALLEY OF DRY BONES

One of the oldest stories in the ancient world is the Egyptian myth of Osiris. According to the legend, Osiris was a great king of Egypt who was murdered by his jealous brother Set. But Set didn't just kill him. He dismembered the body and scattered the pieces across the land. Osiris was not just dead. He was destroyed beyond any possibility of recovery.

His wife, Isis, refused to accept it. She traveled across Egypt, gathering the scattered pieces of his body one by one. When she had found nearly all of theml, she reassembled them, wrapped them in linen, and through magic and mourning, brought Osiris back to a kind of life. He didn't return to the world of the living. Instead, he became the lord of the underworld, ruling over the dead. It was the best the Egyptian imagination could offer: a partial restoration, a shadow of the life that had been lost, a king who could reign only among the dead.

The Egyptians were obsessed with death and resurrection. They built pyramids, mummified bodies, and filled tombs with treasure, all to prepare the dead for a life beyond. But the best they could imagine was Osiris: a reassembled corpse who could rule in the darkness.

Ezekiel 37 imagines something far greater. Not a corpse reassembled for the underworld. Not a shadow of life in the land of the dead. But an entire army of people, long dead, their bones bleached and scattered under the open sky, standing up on their feet, breathing with the breath of God, fully alive, completely restored, and heading home.

This is the most famous chapter in the book of Ezekiel. And it didn't come out of nowhere. It was the climax of a promise that God had been building toward through two full chapters of preparation. Before the bones could live, the enemy had to be dealt with, the land had to be promised, and the people had to be given new hearts.

THE ENEMY SILENCED

Chapter 35 might seem like an interruption. We just finished the beautiful promises of the good shepherd and the covenant of peace. Why go back to another oracle against Edom?

Because the promise of restoration required one more piece of unfinished business. Edom, descended from Esau, Jacob's twin brother, had been Israel's enemy for centuries. That rivalry started in Genesis and never stopped. But what Edom did during the fall of Jerusalem crossed a line that God would not overlook.

When the Babylonians breached Jerusalem's walls, Edom didn't just watch. They celebrated. They mocked. And worst of all, they stationed themselves along the escape routes and attacked Israelite refugees who were fleeing for their lives.

Instead of showing compassion to their distant relatives in their worst moment, the Edomites cut them down as they ran.

God called this "an ancient hostility" and declared that he would make Edom's mountains as desolate as Edom had tried to make Israel's. The nation that had said "these two nations will be ours" (meaning Israel and Judah) would discover that the God of Israel was not dead, not defeated, and not willing to let his people's enemies have the last word.

This mattered for the exiles because it answered a question they must have been asking: if God is going to restore us, what about the people who destroyed us? Are they going to get away with it? The answer was no. Before restoration could begin, the enemies who gloated over Israel's destruction would face their own reckoning.

THE MOUNTAINS WILL SING AGAIN

Chapter 36 is the turning point of the entire book. If the first half of Ezekiel was about tearing down, this chapter is about building up. If chapter 6 pronounced doom on the mountains of Israel, chapter 36 pronounced blessing on those same mountains. The contrast is deliberate. Everything that was destroyed would be restored. Everything that was stripped bare would be made fruitful again.

God addressed the mountains directly: "You will produce branches and fruit for my people Israel, for they will soon come home." The land that had been desolate would be plowed and planted. The cities that had been ruined would be rebuilt and filled with people.

But the physical restoration of the land was only the beginning. God had a deeper problem to address, and it had nothing to do with geography.

"It is not for your sake, people of Israel, that I am going to do these things, but for the sake of my holy name, which you have profaned among the nations."

This is one of the most important theological statements in the entire Old Testament. God was not restoring Israel because they deserved it. They didn't. Their sin had dragged his reputation through the dirt. When the nations looked at Israel's exile, they didn't think, "Israel must have sinned." They thought, "Israel's God must be weak." Every time a pagan neighbor pointed at the scattered, defeated Israelites and said, "So much for the Lord," God's name was being dishonored.

God's motivation for restoration was his own character. He would act to show the nations who he really is. Not because Israel earned it, but because he is who he is.

And what he promised to do was breathtaking.

A NEW HEART

"I will sprinkle clean water on you, and you will be clean. I will cleanse you from all your impurities and from all your idols." Cleansing. A fresh start. Not just forgiveness for past sins, but actual purification, like a priest being washed before entering the temple.

"I will give you a new heart and put a new spirit in you. I will remove from you your heart of stone and give you a heart of flesh." A heart transplant. Not a minor adjustment. Not a self-improvement program. God was going to reach into his people and remove the hard, dead, unresponsive thing that had been beating in their chests and replace it with something alive, soft, and responsive. The old heart that refused to obey, that chased after idols, that wouldn't listen to the prophets, that heart was going to be taken out. A new one was going in.

"And I will put my Spirit in you and move you to follow my decrees and be careful to keep my laws." This was the promise that changed everything. Not just new rules. Not just better instructions. God's own Spirit, living inside his people, giving them the ability to do what they had never been able to do on their own. For the entire history we've walked through in this book, Israel's fundamental problem was an inability to obey. They knew the law. They had the prophets. They had the temple. And still they rebelled, generation after generation after generation. The heart of stone wouldn't respond.

God's solution wasn't to try harder with external commands. It was to change the people from the inside out. New heart. New Spirit. New capacity to love and obey the God who had loved them all along.

The result? "You will live in the land I gave your ancestors. You will be my people, and I will be your God." The covenant formula, the same words God had been saying since Exodus, restored and made permanent. Not because Israel finally got its act together, but because God finally did the surgery that made obedience possible.

The land itself would be transformed. Where there had been desolation, people would say, "This land that was laid waste has become like the garden of Eden." The Garden of Eden. The place where everything began, where God and humanity lived together in unbroken fellowship. The exile had been an expulsion from paradise. The restoration would be a return to it.

CAN THESE BONES LIVE?

Then came the vision. The hand of the Lord was on Ezekiel, and the Spirit carried him out and set him down in the middle of a valley. But this wasn't an ordinary valley. It was full of bones. Human bones. Scattered everywhere, covering the valley floor, bleached white and completely dry. These people hadn't died recently. They had been dead for a very long time. Whatever life had once been in them was utterly gone.

God led Ezekiel back and forth through the valley, making sure he saw the full extent of it. Bones as far as the eye could see. In the ancient world, being left unburied was the ultimate disgrace, the curse pronounced on the worst enemies. These bones represented total, irreversible death.

Then God asked a question that should have had an obvious answer: "Son of man, can these bones live?"

Think about that question for a moment. Look at the scene. Dry bones, scattered in the sun, stripped of every trace of flesh and muscle and breath. Can they live? Logically, medically, scientifically, in every way that a human being would measure such things, the answer was no. Absolutely not. Dead is dead. Bones are bones. You can't undo this.

But Ezekiel had been watching God work for long enough to know better than to answer with human logic. His response was careful, humble, and exactly right: "Sovereign Lord, you alone know."

You alone know. I can't see how it's possible. But I've learned not to put limits on what you can do.

God told Ezekiel to prophesy to the bones. To speak God's word to dead, dry, hopeless remains. "Dry bones, hear the word of the Lord! This is what the Sovereign Lord says to these bones: I will make breath enter you, and you will come to life. I will attach tendons to you and make flesh come upon you and cover you with skin. I will put breath in you, and you will come to life. Then you will know that I am the Lord."

Ezekiel obeyed. He prophesied as he was commanded. And as he spoke, something happened.

A rattling sound. A noise like nothing anyone had ever heard. Bones began to move. They slid across the valley floor, finding their matching pieces, clicking together, skeleton by skeleton. Tendons appeared, stretching across the joints, pulling the frames together. Flesh grew over the tendons. Skin covered the flesh. In moments, the valley floor was covered not with scattered bones but with complete human bodies, thousands upon thousands of them, lying in formation like an army.

But they weren't breathing. The bodies were whole, but they were still dead. Assembled corpses. Like Osiris in the Egyptian myth: put back together, but without real life.

God told Ezekiel to prophesy again, this time to the breath itself. "Come, breath, from the four winds and breathe into these slain, that they may live."

Ezekiel prophesied. And the breath came. It rushed into the bodies, filling lungs that had been empty for years. And they lived. They stood up on their feet, a vast army, alive, breathing, standing.

The vision echoed the creation of the first human being in Genesis, where God formed Adam from the dust of the ground and breathed into his nostrils the breath of life. What God had done for one man at the beginning of creation, he now did for an entire nation at the end of their rope. He re-created them.

THESE BONES ARE MY PEOPLE

God gave Ezekiel the interpretation. "Son of man, these bones are the whole house of Israel. They say, 'Our bones are dried up and our hope is gone; we are cut off.'"

The exiles had been saying exactly that. We're dead. It's over. There's no hope. We've been cut off from God, from the land, from the promises. We might as well be a pile of dry bones in a desert valley.

God's answer was the vision itself. "I am going to open your graves and bring you up from them. I will bring you back to the land of Israel. I will put my Spirit in you and you will live, and I will settle you in your own land. Then you will know that I the Lord have spoken, and I have done it."

The dry bones were not a prophecy about the literal physical resurrection of dead bodies, though later biblical writers would draw on this imagery when talking about resurrection. The dry bones were a picture of the exile itself. Israel was nationally dead. Their identity, their homeland, their temple, their king, everything that made them a people was gone. They were scattered, dry, and hopeless.

And God said: I can fix this. I can bring life out of death. I can take the most hopeless situation you can imagine and reverse it completely. Not because you deserve it. Not because you've figured out how to save yourselves. But because I am the Lord, and nothing is too dead for me to raise.

TWO STICKS, ONE NATION

The chapter closes with one final sign-act, the last one in the entire book. God told Ezekiel to take two sticks. On one he was to write "Judah," representing the southern kingdom. On the other he was to write "Joseph," representing the northern kingdom that had been conquered and scattered by Assyria over a century earlier.

Then Ezekiel was to hold them together in his hand so they became one.

The meaning was clear. Israel had been divided since the days of Solomon's son Rehoboam, when the kingdom split in two. The north was eventually destroyed by Assyria. The south fell to Babylon. For generations, there had been no unified people of God.

God promised to change that. He would take both halves, north and south, and make them one nation again under one king. "My servant David will be king over them, and they will all have one shepherd." The covenant of peace would be everlasting. God's dwelling place would be among them. And the nations would finally know that the Lord makes Israel holy.

"My dwelling place will be with them. I will be their God, and they will be my people."

From the very first pages of Genesis, that had always been the goal. God with his people. Dwelling together. No separation. No exile. No dry bones. Just life, and the presence of the God who gives it.

WHAT THIS MEANS FOR US

First, no situation is too hopeless for God. The dry bones were as dead as dead gets. There was zero natural possibility of life returning. And God brought them back anyway. Whatever feels dead in your life, whatever situation seems permanently beyond repair, God specializes in the impossible. Don't measure what God can do by what you can see.

Second, real change comes from the inside out. God didn't give Israel a better set of rules or a more motivating speech. He gave them a new heart and his own Spirit. That's the same thing he offers you. The Christian life isn't about trying harder with the same old heart. It's about receiving a new one, and letting God's Spirit do in you what you could never do on your own.

Third, God acts for the sake of his name, not our merit. Israel didn't earn restoration. God restored them because his reputation was at stake. This is actually better news than if it depended on us. If God's commitment to us were based on our performance, we'd be in trouble. But because it's based on his character, it's unshakable.

Fourth, God's ultimate goal is to dwell with his people. The chapter builds toward one destination: "My dwelling place will be with them." Every promise of new hearts, gathered exiles, united kingdoms, and peaceful covenants points to this single reality. God wants to be with his people. And through Jesus and the Holy Spirit, he has made that possible for anyone who trusts him.

TALKING POINTS

1. **God asked Ezekiel, "Can these bones live?" and Ezekiel answered, "Sovereign Lord, you alone know."** Why do you think Ezekiel answered that way instead of saying yes or no? What does his answer teach us about the right way to approach situations that seem impossible?

2. **God said he was restoring Israel "not for your sake, but for the sake of my holy name."** Does it bother you that God's primary motivation wasn't Israel's comfort but his own glory? Why or why not? How is this actually more comforting than if restoration depended on Israel's merit?

3. **The promise of a "new heart" and "new spirit" means that God does the work of transformation inside us.** How does this change the way you think about the Christian life? Is it more about effort or surrender? What's the difference between trying to change yourself and letting God change you?

4. **The dry bones vision showed bodies being reassembled and then receiving breath.** Why do you think it happened in two stages? What's the difference between having the right "structure" in your life (going to church, knowing the rules) and having the breath of God actually living inside you?

5. **The two sticks being joined into one represented a divided nation being reunited.** What does division look like among God's people today? What would it take for the kind of unity God described here to become a reality?

The bones had risen. The breath had entered. The sticks were joined. The covenant of peace was promised. For the first time since the opening chapters of this dark, devastating book, the future looked like something other than destruction.

But God wasn't finished. One more vision remained, the longest and strangest of them all. Ezekiel would be taken to a mountain and shown a temple unlike anything that had ever existed, a place where the glory of God would return and a river of life would flow from the throne. The story of Ezekiel would end where it began: with the glory of the Lord.

Turn the page.

10

THE GLORY RETURNS

Homer's *Odyssey* is the story of the longest journey home in all of literature. After fighting in the Trojan War for ten years, the Greek hero Odysseus spends another ten years trying to get back to his island of Ithaca. He battles a one-eyed giant. He resists enchantresses. He sails past monsters and through deadly whirlpools. He loses every one of his ships and every one of his men. He washes up on foreign shores, is held captive by a goddess, and nearly drowns more than once. For twenty years, his wife Penelope waits. His son Telemachus grows up without a father. And through all of it, one desire drives Odysseus forward: home. He just wants to go home.

When he finally reaches Ithaca, the story isn't over. His house has been overrun by enemies who have been eating his food, courting his wife, and disrespecting his legacy. Odysseus has to fight one more battle to reclaim what belongs to him. But when the battle is won and the enemies are defeated, he is home. Truly, finally home.

The book of Ezekiel ends with a homecoming. Not a human hero returning to a human city, but something infinitely greater: the glory of God returning to dwell with his people. After forty-eight chapters of visions, sign-acts, judgments, and promises, after the glory departed from the temple and the city was burned and the people were scattered, God comes back. And this time, he comes back to stay.

THE LAST BATTLE

Before the homecoming, there was one more threat to face.

Chapters 38 and 39 describe an attack on the restored people of Israel by a mysterious figure called Gog, from the land of Magog. Nobody knows exactly who Gog was. Some have connected the name to Gyges, an ancient king of Lydia. Others think the name is intentionally vague, representing a future enemy so distant and unknown that Ezekiel's audience couldn't identify him. What's clear is that Gog represents the ultimate threat: a massive coalition of nations from the farthest corners of the known world, descending on God's peaceful, restored people with overwhelming force.

The geography is deliberately wide. Gog's allies come from Meshek and Tubal in Asia Minor, Persia to the east, Cush in Africa, Put in Libya, Gomer and Beth Togarmah in the far north. This isn't one nation attacking another. This is the whole world converging on Israel. The attack comes "like a cloud covering the land," a force so enormous it darkens the sky.

But here's the detail that changes everything: God is the one who brings Gog. "I will put hooks in your jaws and bring you out," God says, using the same language he used for Pharaoh back in chapter 29. Gog thinks he's launching a brilliant military campaign against an undefended target. In reality,

God is drawing him into a trap. The battle isn't between Gog and Israel. It's between Gog and God. And it isn't close.

God destroys Gog with earthquake, plague, bloodshed, torrential rain, hailstones, and burning sulfur. The weapons of the defeated army are so numerous that Israel uses them for fuel for seven years. The dead are so many that it takes seven months to bury them all, and even after that, search parties continue combing the land for any remaining bones. The land must be completely cleansed.

The purpose of the battle is stated repeatedly: "I will display my glory among the nations." The defeat of Gog is the final demonstration that Israel's God is the sovereign ruler of all nations, all armies, and all history. The exile was not a sign of God's weakness. It was a consequence of Israel's sin. And now that the sin has been dealt with and the people have been restored, no force on earth can threaten what God has established.

The book of Revelation picks up this imagery directly. In Revelation 20, after a long period of Christ's reign, Satan gathers the nations for one final assault on God's people. The nations are called "Gog and Magog." And just as in Ezekiel, fire comes down from heaven and destroys them. Ezekiel's vision of the last battle became the template for the Bible's final vision of evil's ultimate defeat.

THE TEMPLE THAT NEVER WAS

In the twenty-fifth year of the exile, fourteen years after Jerusalem fell, Ezekiel received his final vision. The Spirit set him on a very high mountain in the land of Israel, and below him he saw what looked like a city. A figure like a man, shining like bronze, stood at the gate holding a measuring rod and a linen cord. And for the next nine chapters, this angelic guide walked Ezekiel through the most detailed architectural vision in the Bible.

The temple was enormous. The outer court, the inner court, the gates with their guard alcoves, the storage rooms, the kitchens for preparing sacrifices, the chambers for priests to change their clothes. Every measurement was recorded. Every dimension was precise. The symmetry was perfect, communicating an order and beauty that reflected the character of the God who designed it.

But this temple was different from Solomon's in ways that go beyond size. No ark of the covenant is mentioned. The layout doesn't match the instructions Moses received at Sinai or the design Solomon built in Jerusalem. The land divisions described in chapter 48 don't correspond to the actual geography of Israel. The river that flows from the temple in chapter 47, growing deeper and wider until it reaches the Dead Sea and turns its salt water fresh, doesn't behave like any natural river. Trees on its banks bear fruit every month, and their leaves are for healing.

Something unusual is happening in these chapters. Ezekiel is using the language of physical architecture and real geography to describe a reality that goes beyond anything that could be built with human hands. The measurements communicate perfection. The river communicates life flowing from God's presence into every dead and desolate place. The land divisions communicate fairness and wholeness. And the whole vision builds toward a single, climactic moment.

THE GLORY COMES HOME

The guide brought Ezekiel to the east gate of the temple. And there, coming from the east, Ezekiel saw the glory of the God of Israel.

The sound of it was like the roar of rushing waters. The land was radiant with his brilliance. Ezekiel recognized it immediately. It was the same glory he had seen in his very first vision by the Kebar canal, the same glory he had watched depart from the temple in chapters 8–11, moving reluctantly from the ark to the threshold to the east gate to the Mount of Olives before vanishing.

Now it was coming back. Through the same east gate. In the same direction. The glory that had left was returning.

"The glory of the Lord entered the temple through the gate facing east. Then the Spirit lifted me up and brought me into the inner court, and the glory of the Lord filled the temple."

For the exiles who had listened to Ezekiel describe the glory's departure, this was the moment that made everything else worthwhile. The temple without God's glory was just a building. The city without God's presence was just a ruin. But God was coming back. And this time, the east gate was permanently sealed behind him. He wasn't leaving again. Ever.

From inside the temple, God spoke: "Son of man, this is the place of my throne and the place for the soles of my feet. This is where I will live among the Israelites forever."

Forever. Not temporarily. Not conditionally. Not "until you mess up again." Forever.

THE RIVER OF LIFE

One of the most beautiful images in the entire Bible appears in chapter 47. Ezekiel was brought back to the entrance of the temple, and he saw water trickling out from under the threshold, flowing east. The guide led him along the stream. At first the water was ankle-deep. A thousand cubits further, it reached the knees. Another thousand, the waist. And a thousand more, it was a river too deep to cross, a river you could only swim in.

The water flowed down toward the Dead Sea, the lowest point on earth, a body of water so saturated with salt that nothing can live in it. No fish. No plants. Nothing. The Dead Sea was the biblical image of complete lifelessness.

And when the river from the temple reached it, the salt water became fresh. Fish filled the waters. Fishermen lined the shores. "Swarms of living creatures will live wherever the river flows." On both banks, fruit trees grew, bearing fresh fruit every month, their leaves providing healing.

This wasn't a description of a plumbing project. This was a vision of what happens when God's presence flows into the world. Life. Healing. Fruitfulness. Even the deadest, most hopeless place on earth is transformed when the river of God reaches it.

The New Testament recognized this immediately. Jesus stood in the temple during the Festival of Tabernacles and declared, "Let anyone who is thirsty come to me and drink. Whoever believes in me, rivers of living water will flow from within them." John explained that Jesus was talking about the Holy Spirit. And in the very last chapter of the Bible, Revelation 22, John saw "the river of the water of life, as clear as crystal, flowing from the throne of God and of the Lamb," with trees on either side bearing fruit every month, their leaves "for the healing of the nations."

Ezekiel's river and Revelation's river are the same river. The life that flows from God's presence, first pictured in a visionary temple on a high mountain, finds its ultimate fulfillment in the new creation, where God dwells with his people and everything dead is made alive.

THE CITY'S NAME

The final chapter of Ezekiel divided the restored land among the twelve tribes of Israel in a pattern of perfect symmetry. Seven tribes to the north, five to the south, with a sacred district in the center containing the temple, the priestly territory, and a city.

The city had twelve gates, three on each side, named for the twelve sons of Jacob. Every tribe had access. No one was excluded. The gates of Revelation's New Jerusalem, described in Revelation 21, follow the same pattern: twelve gates, twelve tribes, open access for God's people from every direction.

But the most important detail was saved for the very last line of the book. After forty-eight chapters, after visions of wheels and fire and living creatures, after sign-acts and sieges and shaved heads, after the glory departed and the city burned, after dry bones and new hearts and rivers of life, Ezekiel ended his book with a single sentence about the name of the city.

"And the name of the city from that time on will be: THE LORD IS THERE."

That's it. That's what everything has been leading to. Not the size of the temple or the precision of the measurements or the symmetry of the land divisions. The point of the whole book, from the first verse to the last, is presence. God's presence.

The book began with Ezekiel sitting in exile, wondering if God had abandoned his people. It ends with a city whose very name declares that he never will again. The glory that departed has returned. The God who seemed absent is permanently, irrevocably, eternally present.

The Lord is there.

WHAT THIS MEANS FOR US

First, no enemy can ultimately defeat what God has established. Gog brought the armies of the whole world against God's people, and God destroyed them without Israel lifting a finger. Whatever threatens you, whatever forces seem arrayed against your faith, the final chapter has already been written. God wins.

Second, God's presence is the point of everything. The temple vision wasn't ultimately about architecture. The land divisions weren't about geography. The river wasn't about water. Everything pointed to one reality: God dwelling with his people. That's what heaven is. That's what the church is meant to be. That's what the Christian life is about. Not rules or rituals or religious activity, but the living presence of God, flowing through his people like a river that brings life to every dead place it touches.

Third, the story of Ezekiel is the story of the whole Bible. Creation began in a garden where God walked with humans. Sin drove them out. The rest of Scripture is the story of God working to bring them back. The tabernacle, the temple, the incarnation of Jesus, the gift of the Holy Spirit, the promise of a new heaven and new earth: all of it points to the same destination. God with us. That's where the story ends. Not in exile. Not in destruction. In presence.

Fourth, the river flows outward. The water didn't stay in the temple. It flowed out, gaining depth and power, reaching the deadest place on earth and bringing it to life. God's presence isn't meant to be contained in a building or hoarded by a community. It's meant to flow outward, reaching people and places that seem beyond hope, and transforming them.

TALKING POINTS

1. **The battle with Gog was entirely God's fight. Israel didn't need to lift a weapon.** What does this teach you about the difference between battles you need to fight yourself and battles you need to trust God to fight for you?

2. **The temple vision is full of precise measurements and perfect symmetry.** Why do you think God used architectural language to communicate spiritual realities? What does the perfection of the temple tell us about God's character?

3. **The glory of God returned through the same east gate it had departed from.** Why do you think this detail matters? What does it tell us about God's faithfulness and his willingness to come back to places he has left?

4. **The river from the temple turned the Dead Sea into a place teeming with life.** Where are the "Dead Sea" places in your world, the situations or relationships that seem completely lifeless? How might God's presence bring unexpected life to those places?

5. The book ends with the name of the city: "THE LORD IS THERE." If you could rename your school, your home, or your community based on what you want to be true about it, what name would you give it? What would it take for "The Lord is there" to be the defining truth of your life?

The book of Ezekiel began in exile, beside a muddy canal in Babylon, with a young priest who thought his life was over. It ends on a mountaintop, overlooking a city whose name means "The Lord is there."

Between those two points lies the most devastating and the most hopeful journey in all of Scripture. A nation destroyed and rebuilt. A temple emptied and filled again. A people given hearts of stone replaced with hearts of flesh. Dry bones brought to life. A river flowing from the throne of God into the deadest place on earth, making everything it touches alive.

The glory departed. The glory returned. And this time, it will never leave.

www.ingramcontent.com/pod-product-compliance
Lightning Source LLC
Chambersburg PA
CBHW050951050726
47592CB00007B/2527